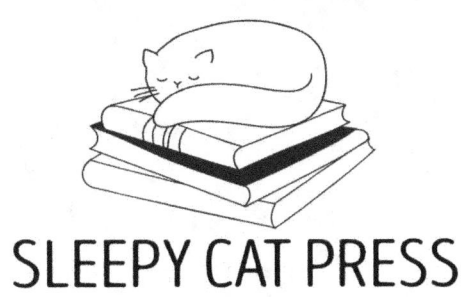

SLEEPY CAT PRESS

Presents

SPOOKY HALLOWEEN FACES

50 Pages of Unique Halloween Faces to Color

Volume 1

www.sleepycatpress.com

SPOOKY HALLOWEEN FACES

All rights reserved. No portion of this book may be reproduced in any form without permission from the publisher, except as permitted by U.S. copyright law.

First Edition September 2022

Design and layout by Horace Sweat.

ISBN: 9798848452976

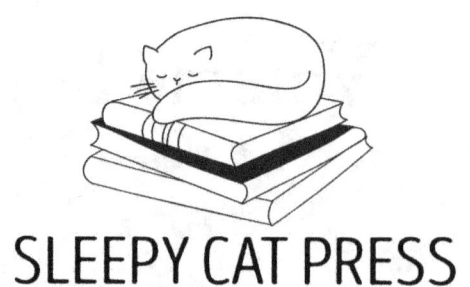

SLEEPY CAT PRESS

Copyright © 2022 Sleepy Cat Press

All rights reserved.

Dedicated to Miss. Maya, who loved to color.

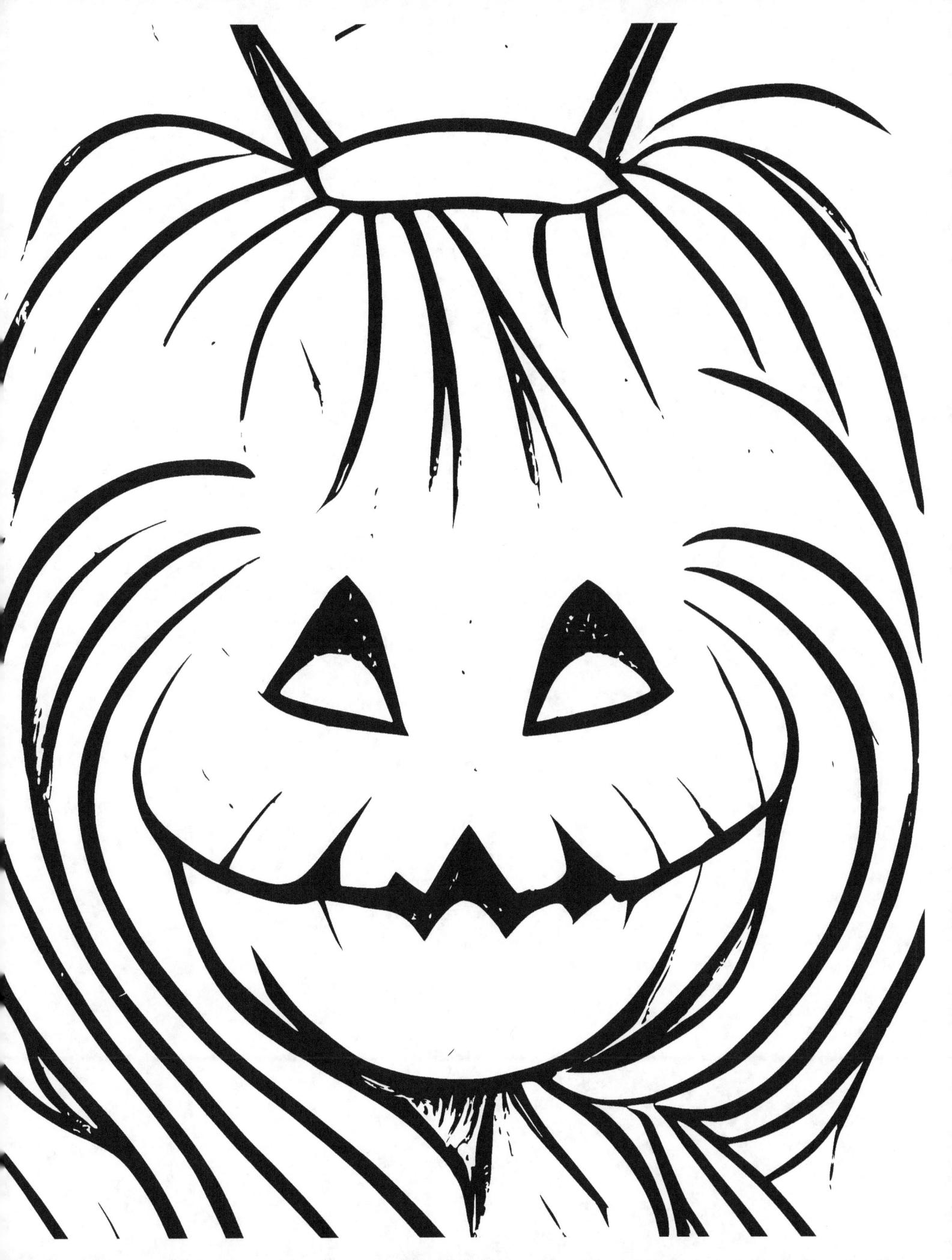

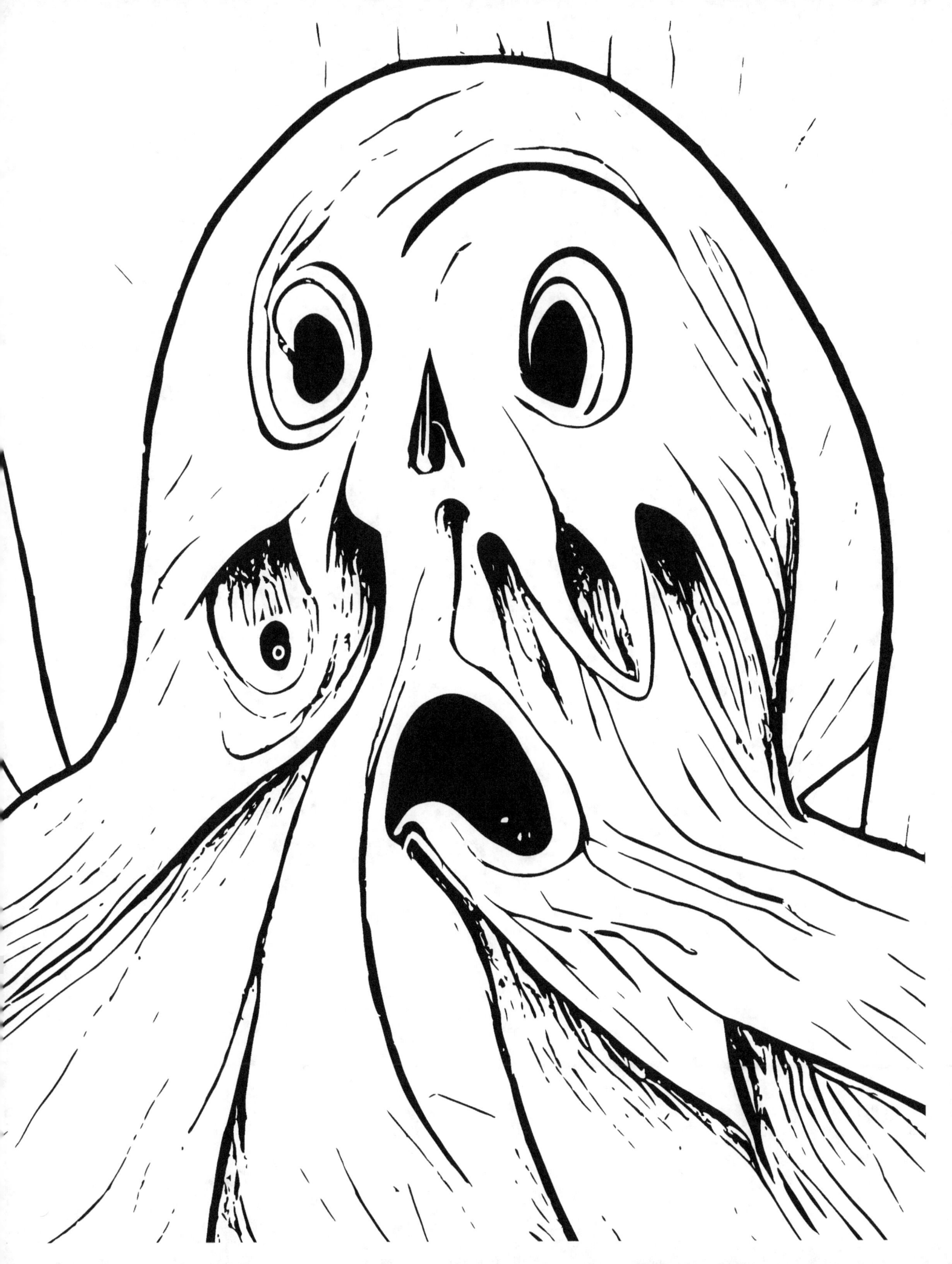

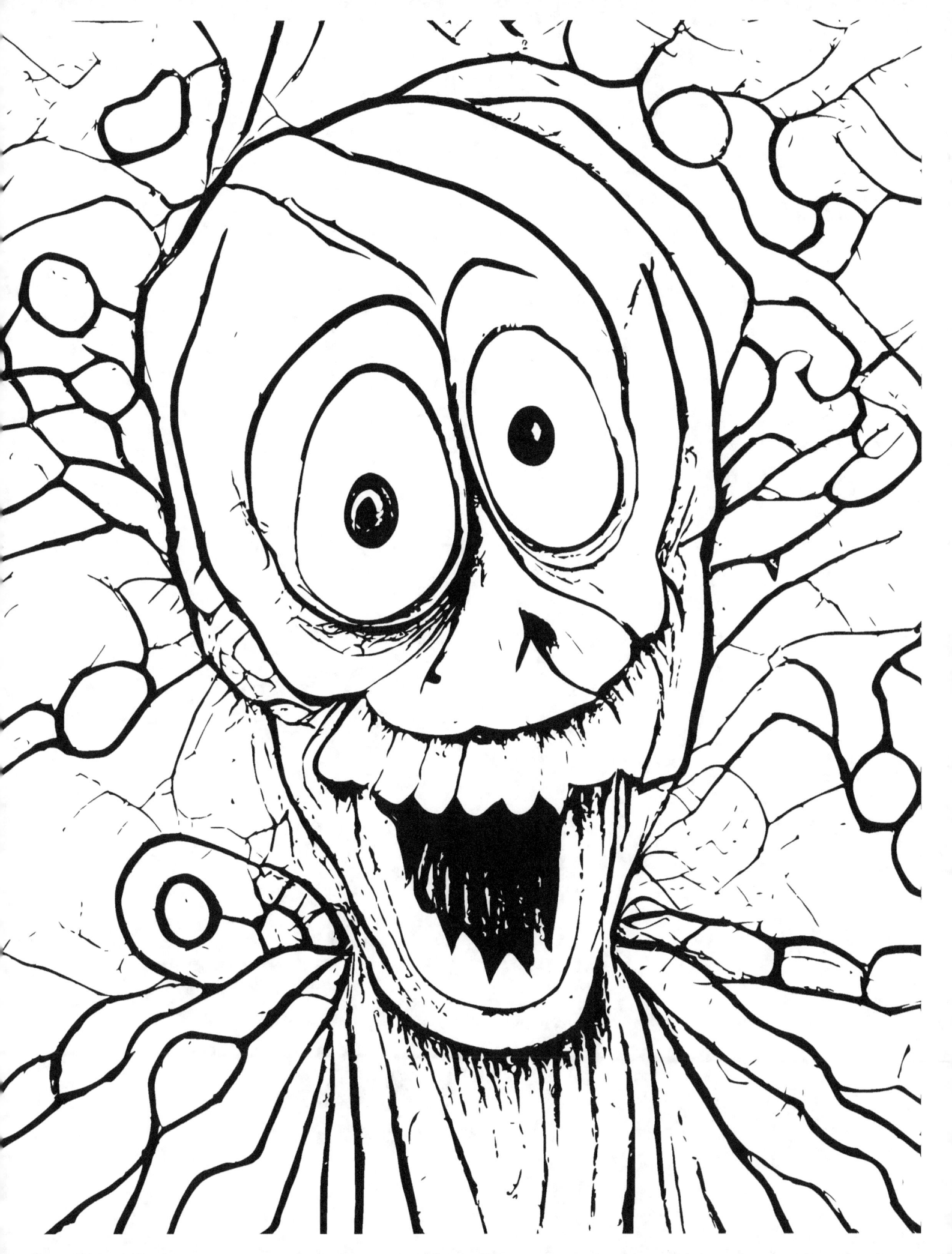

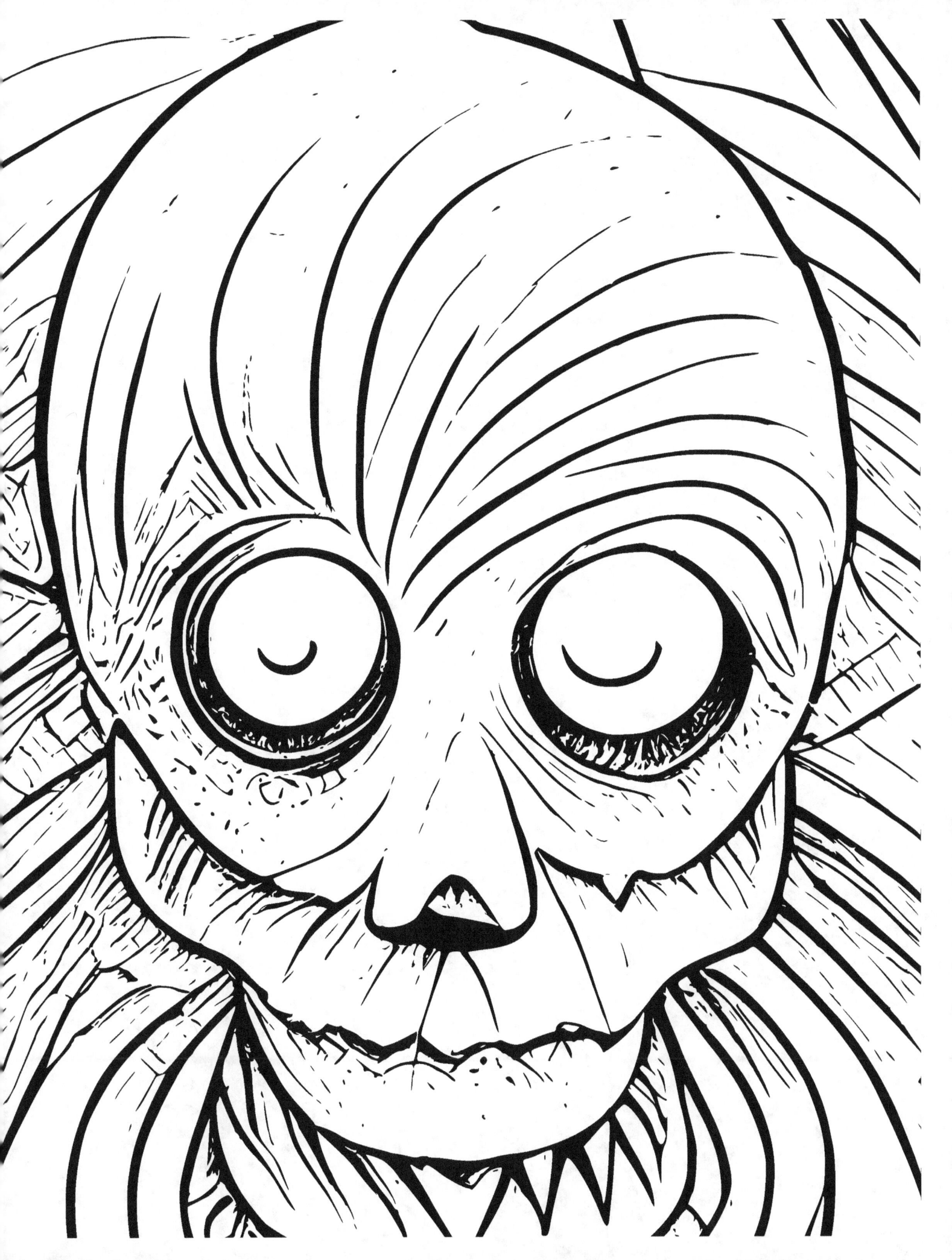

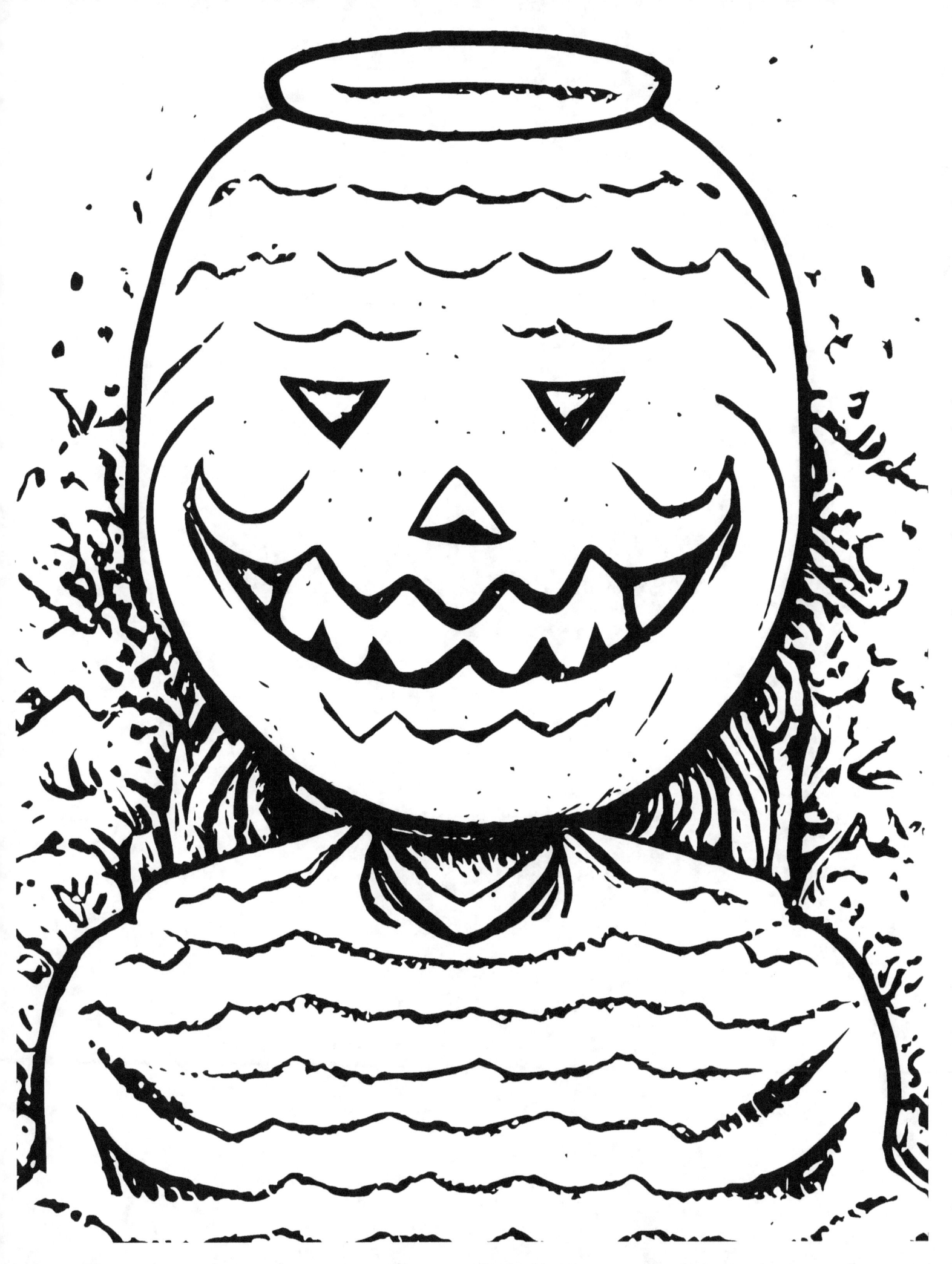

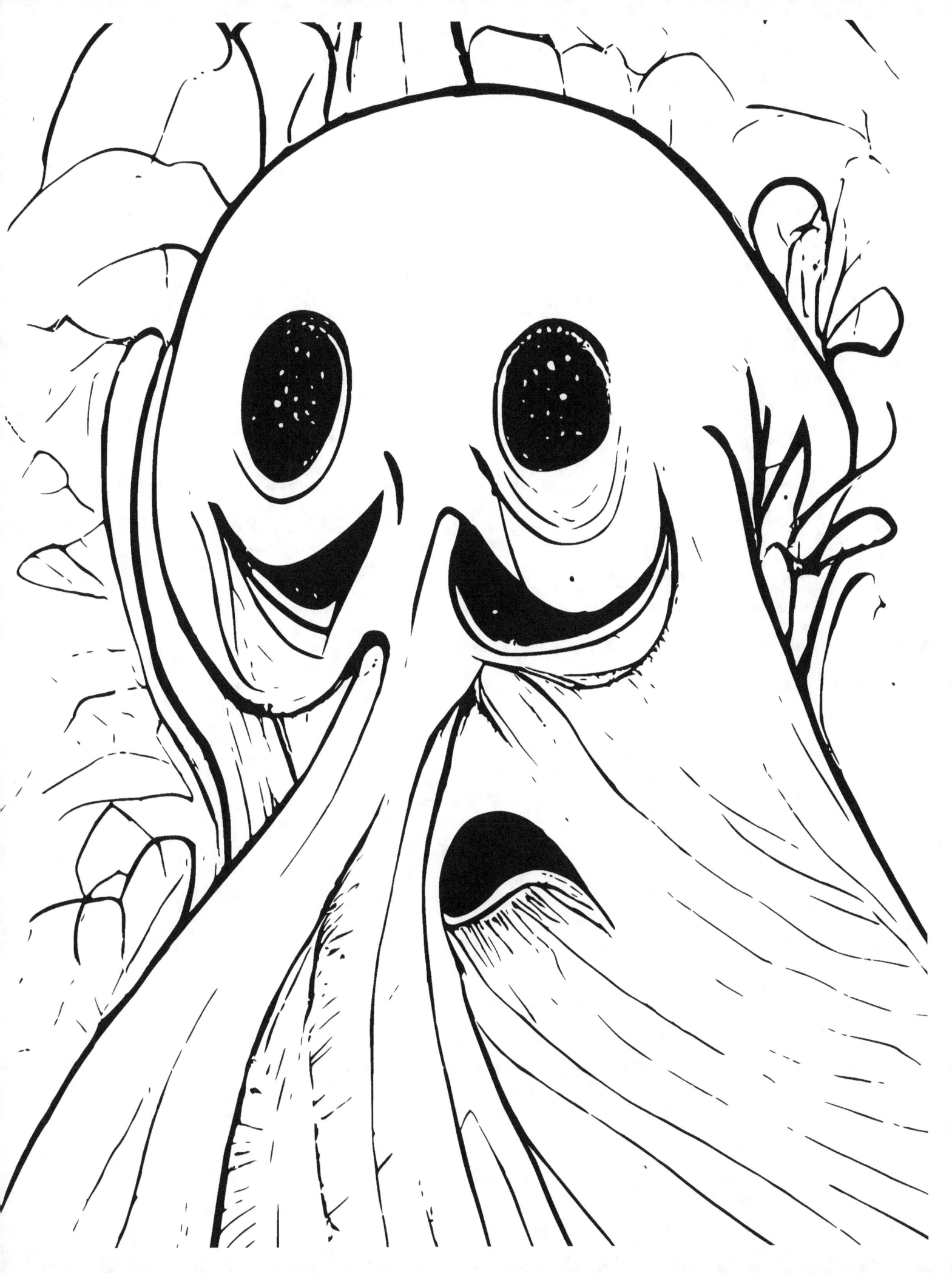

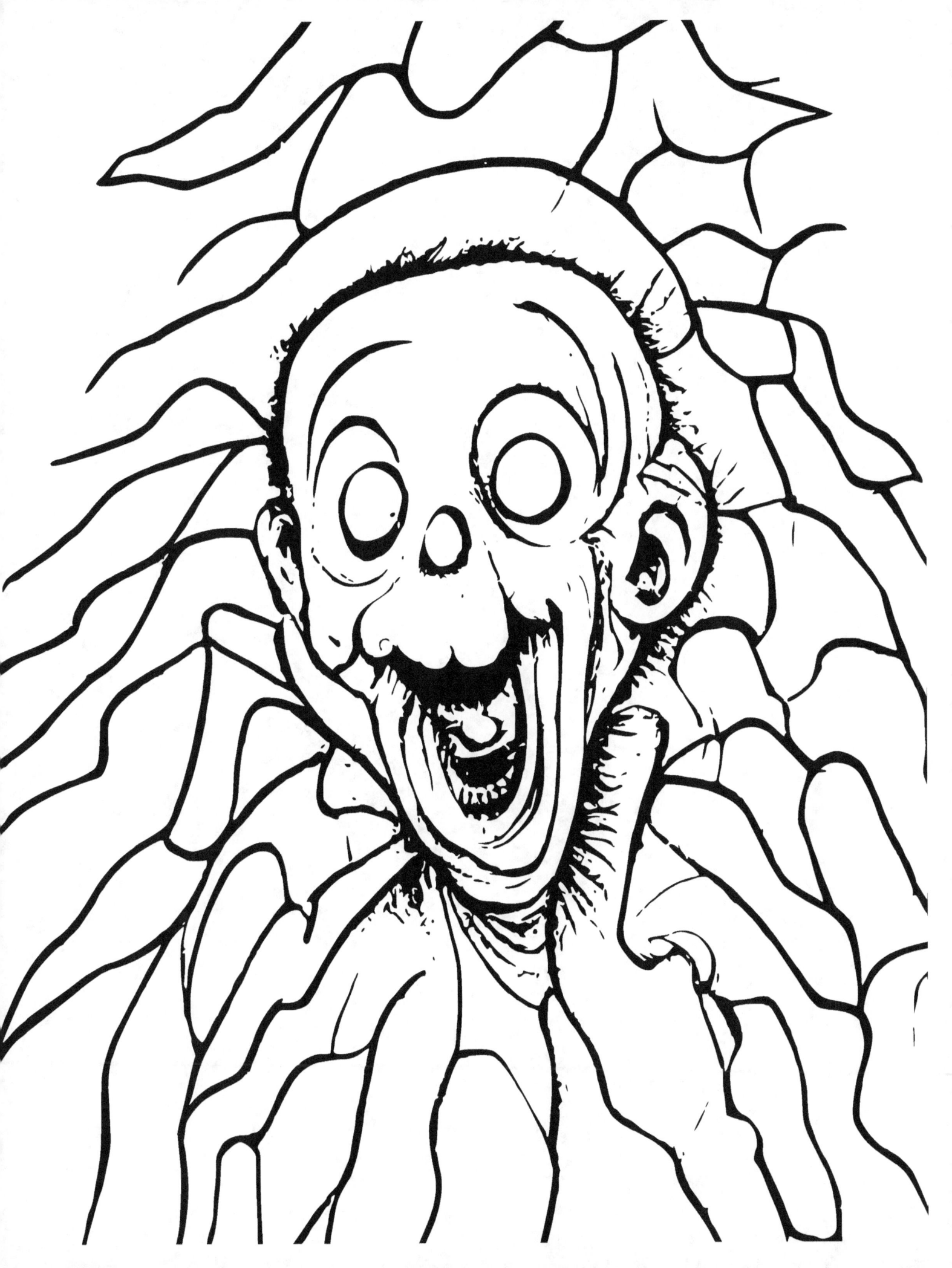

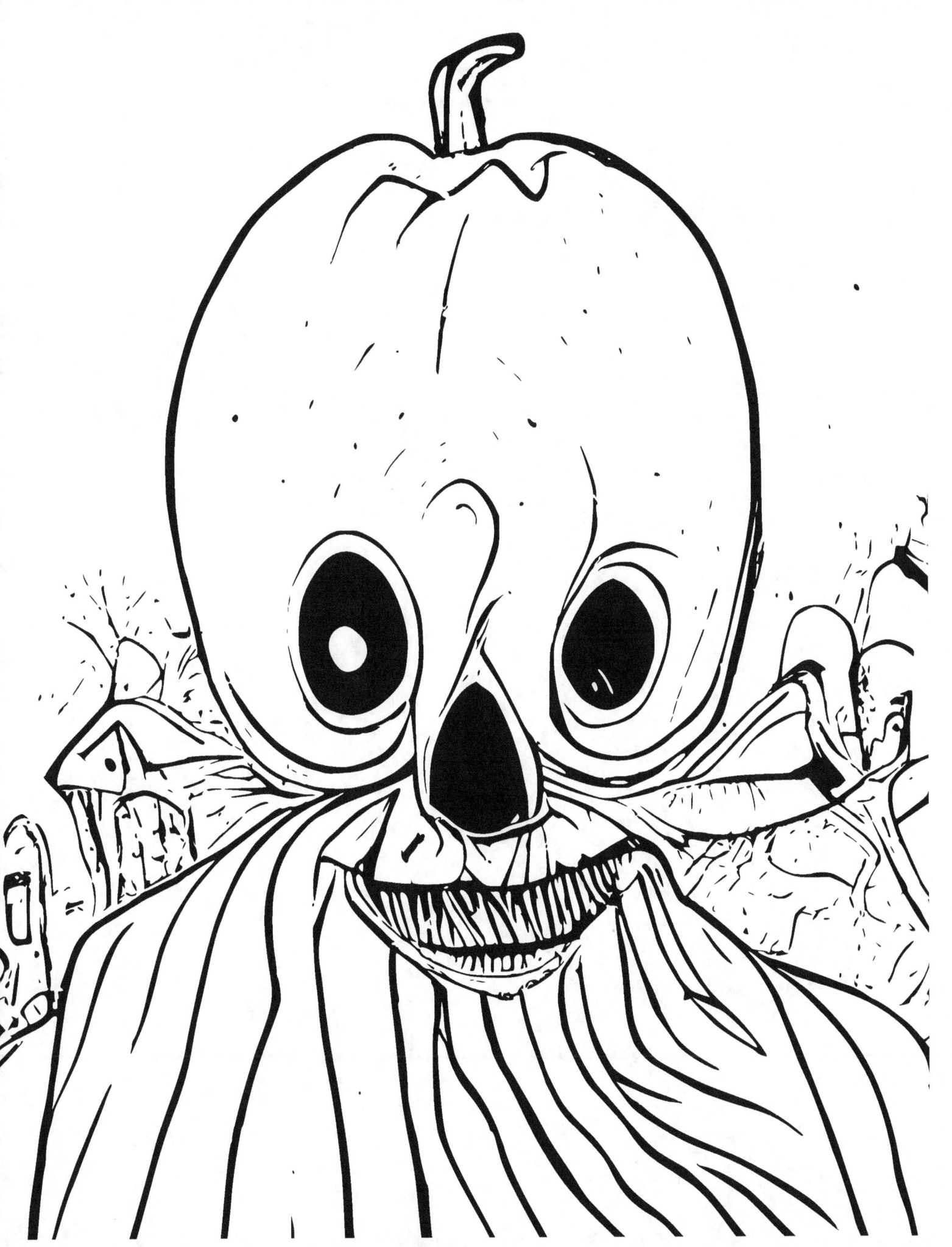

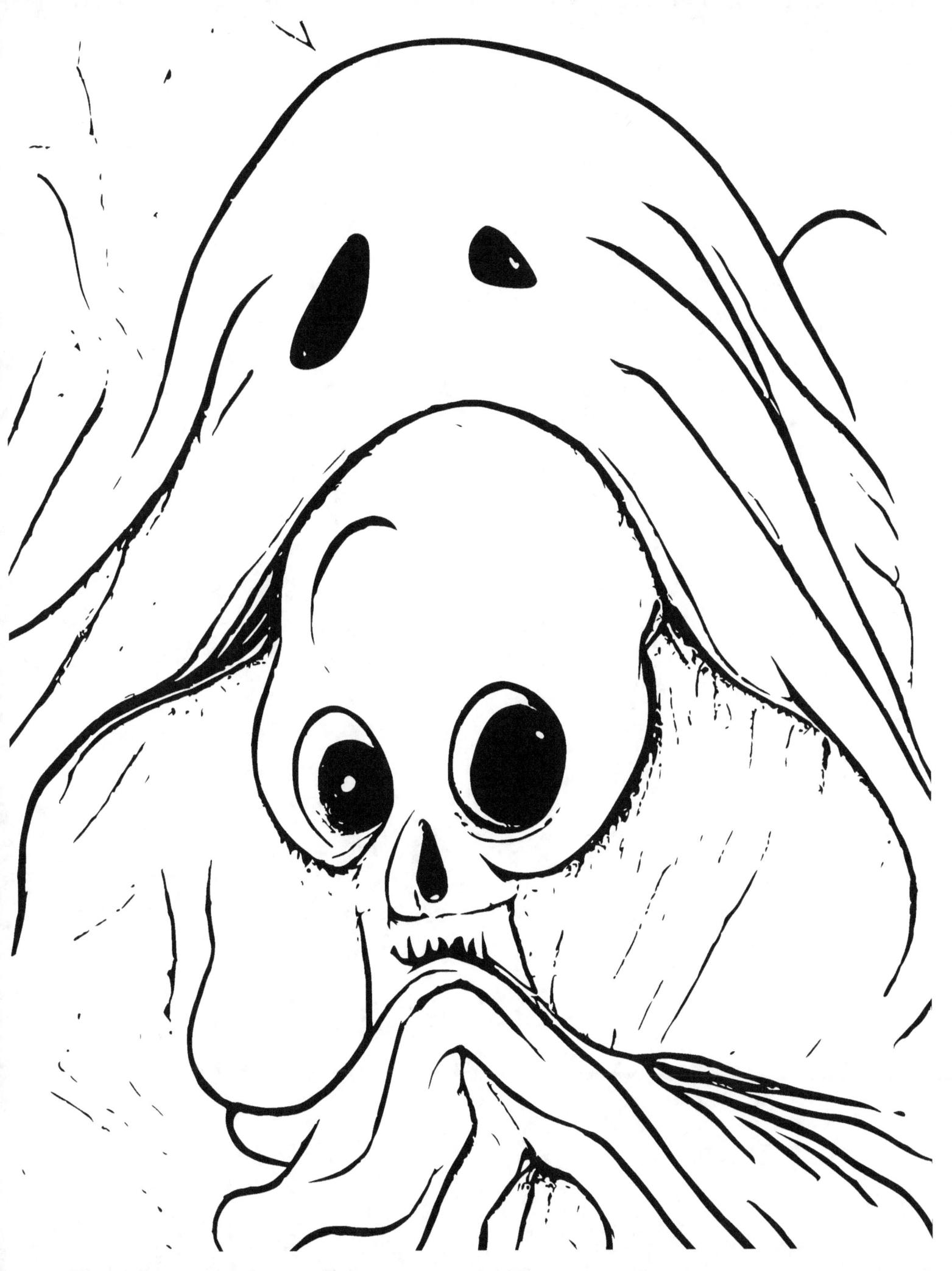

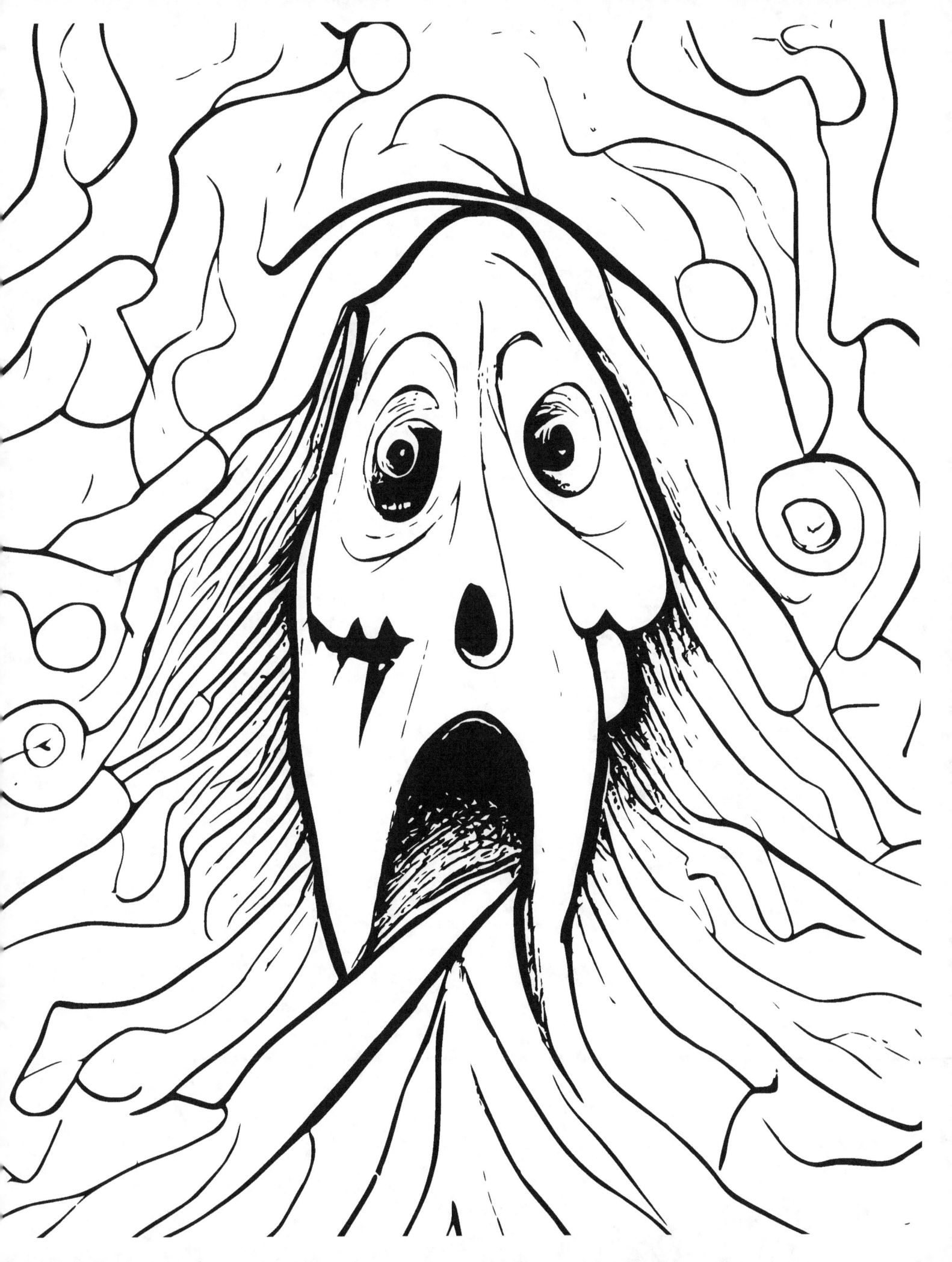

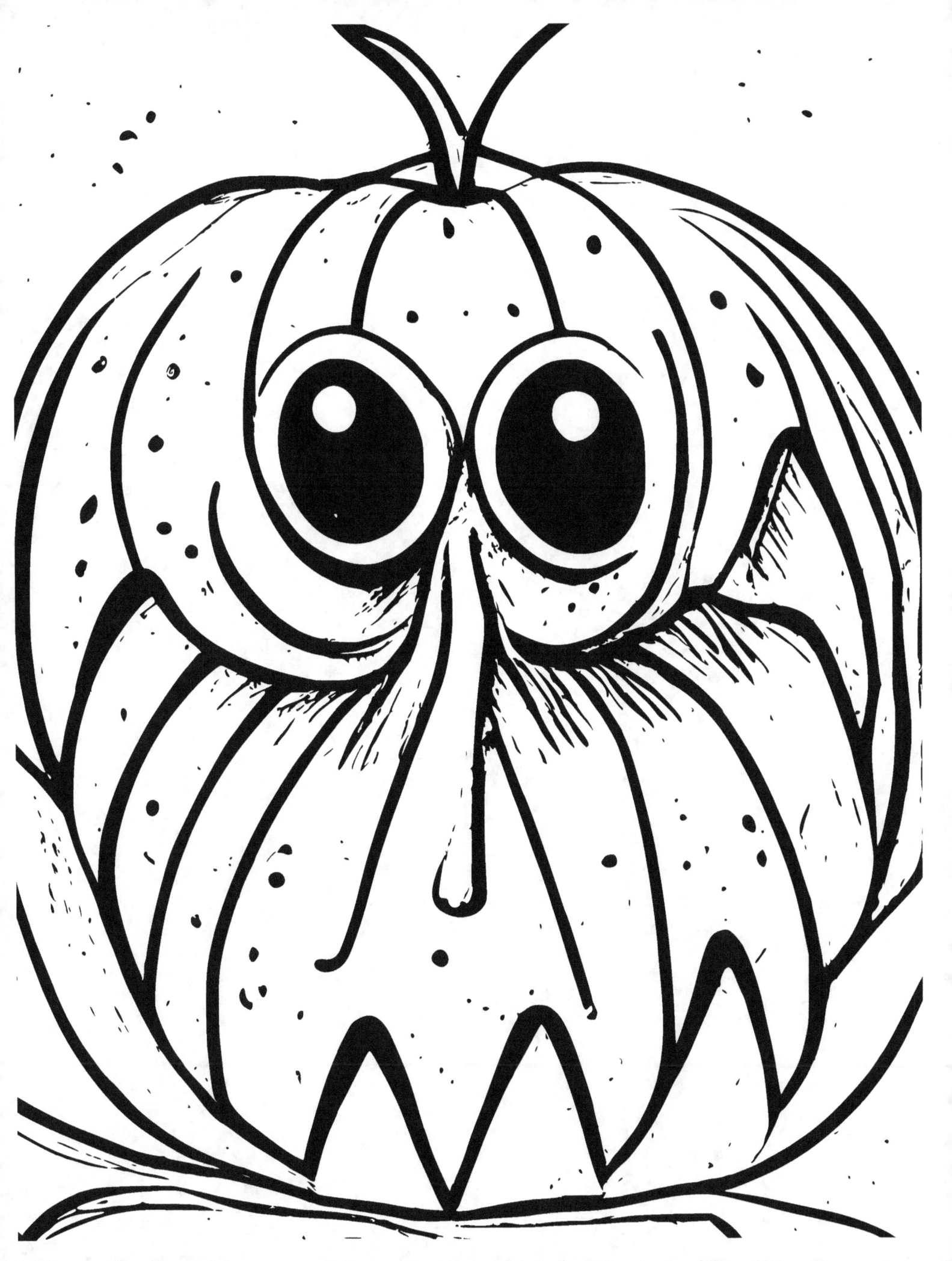

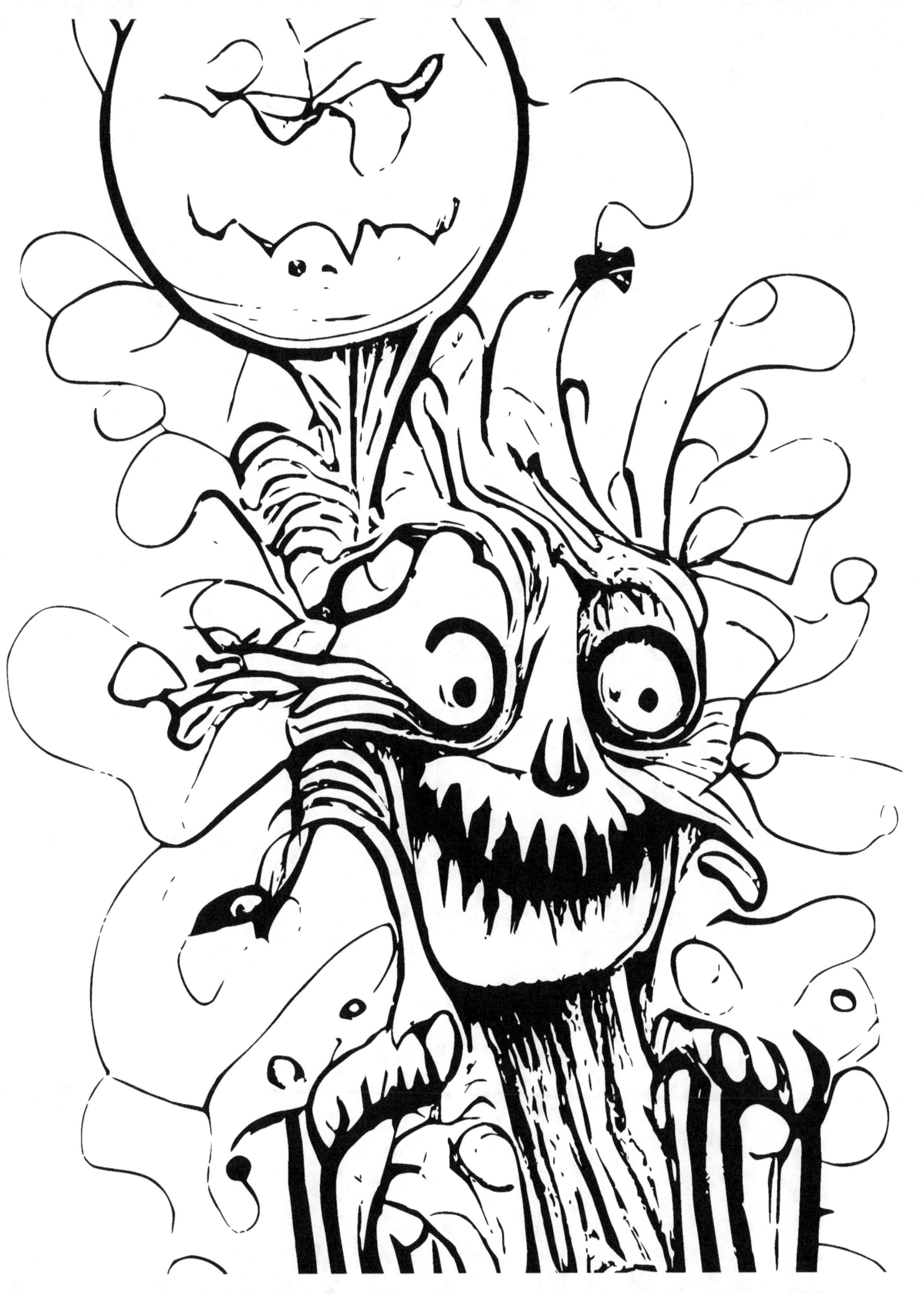

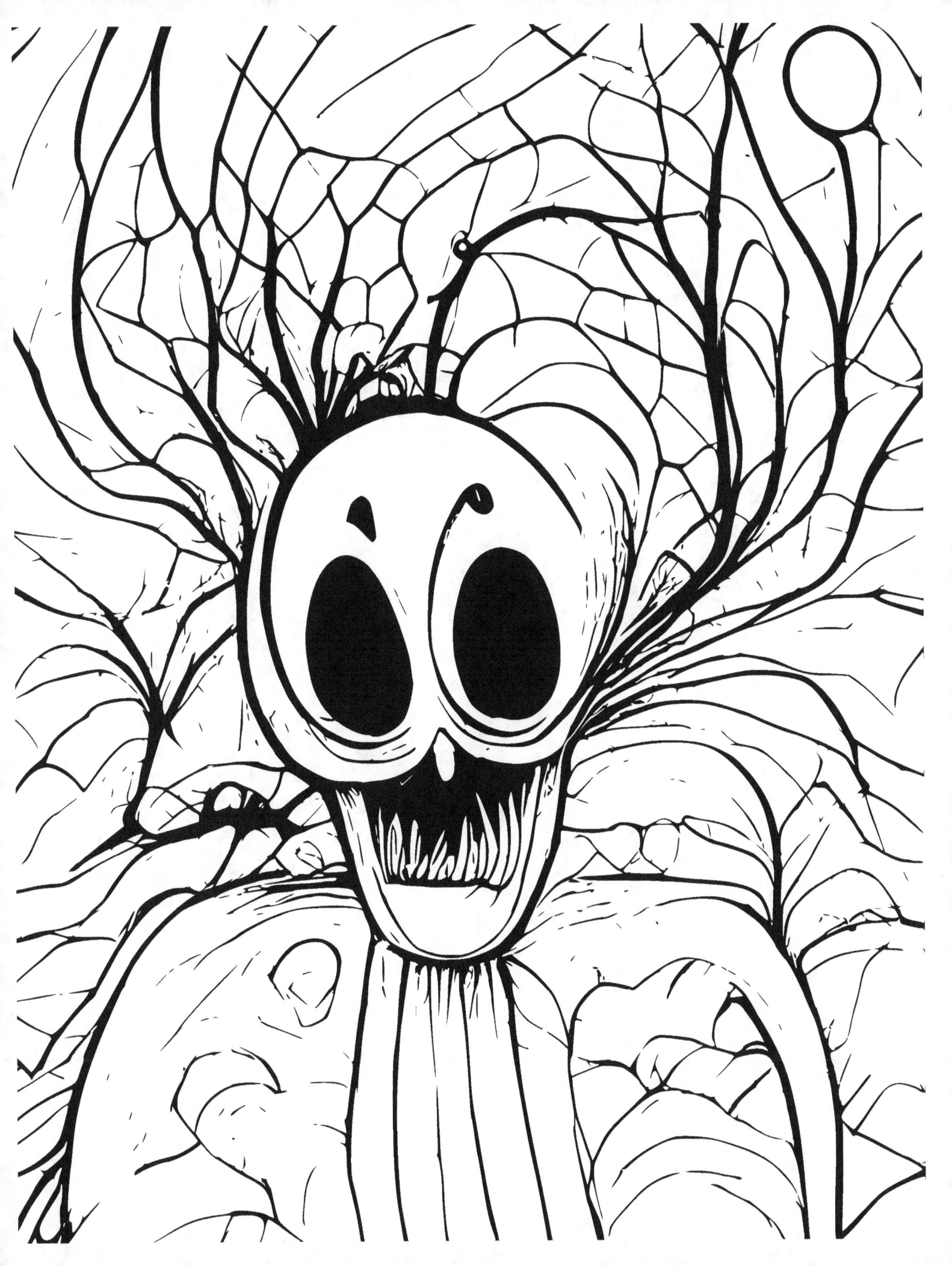

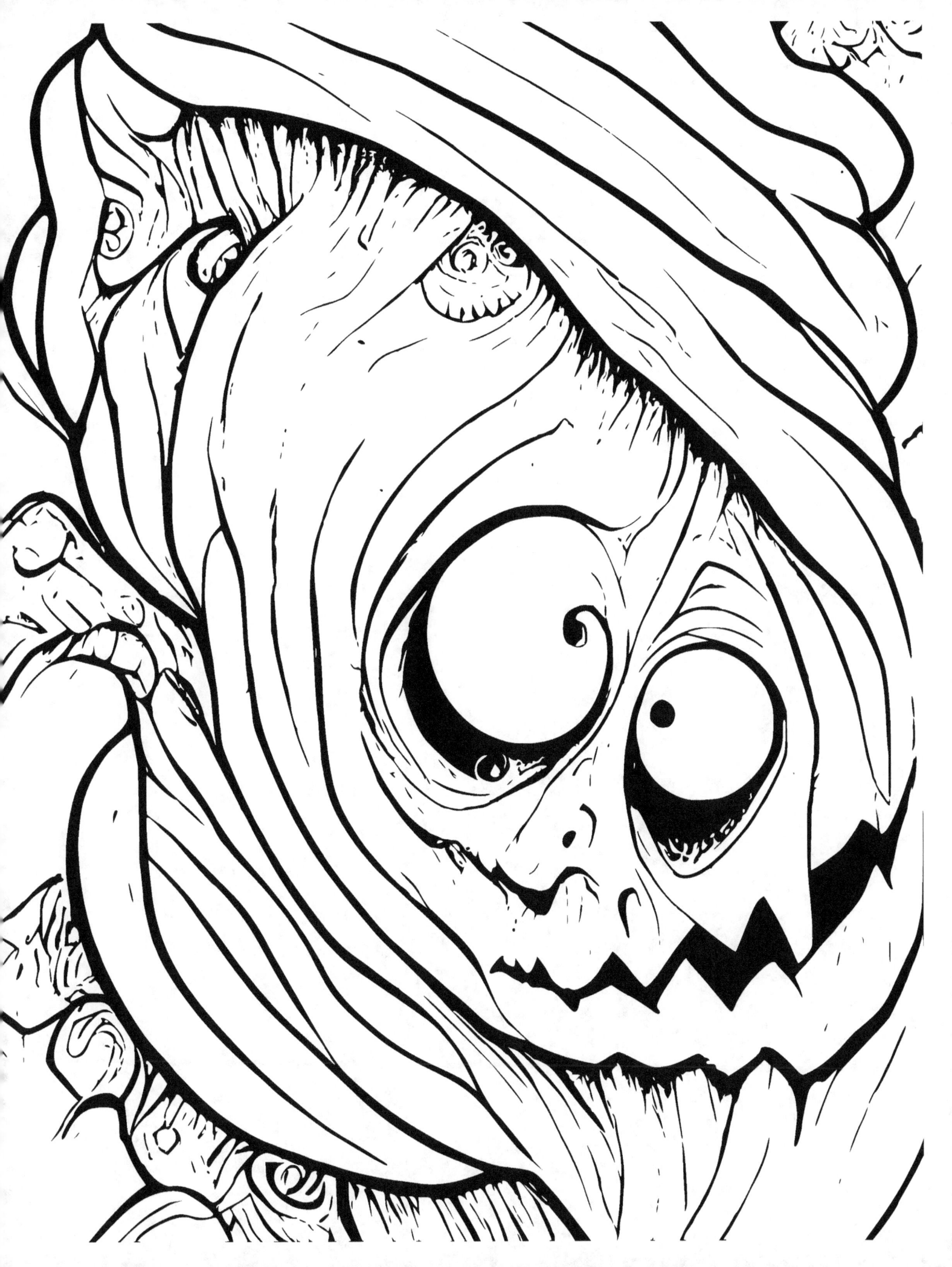

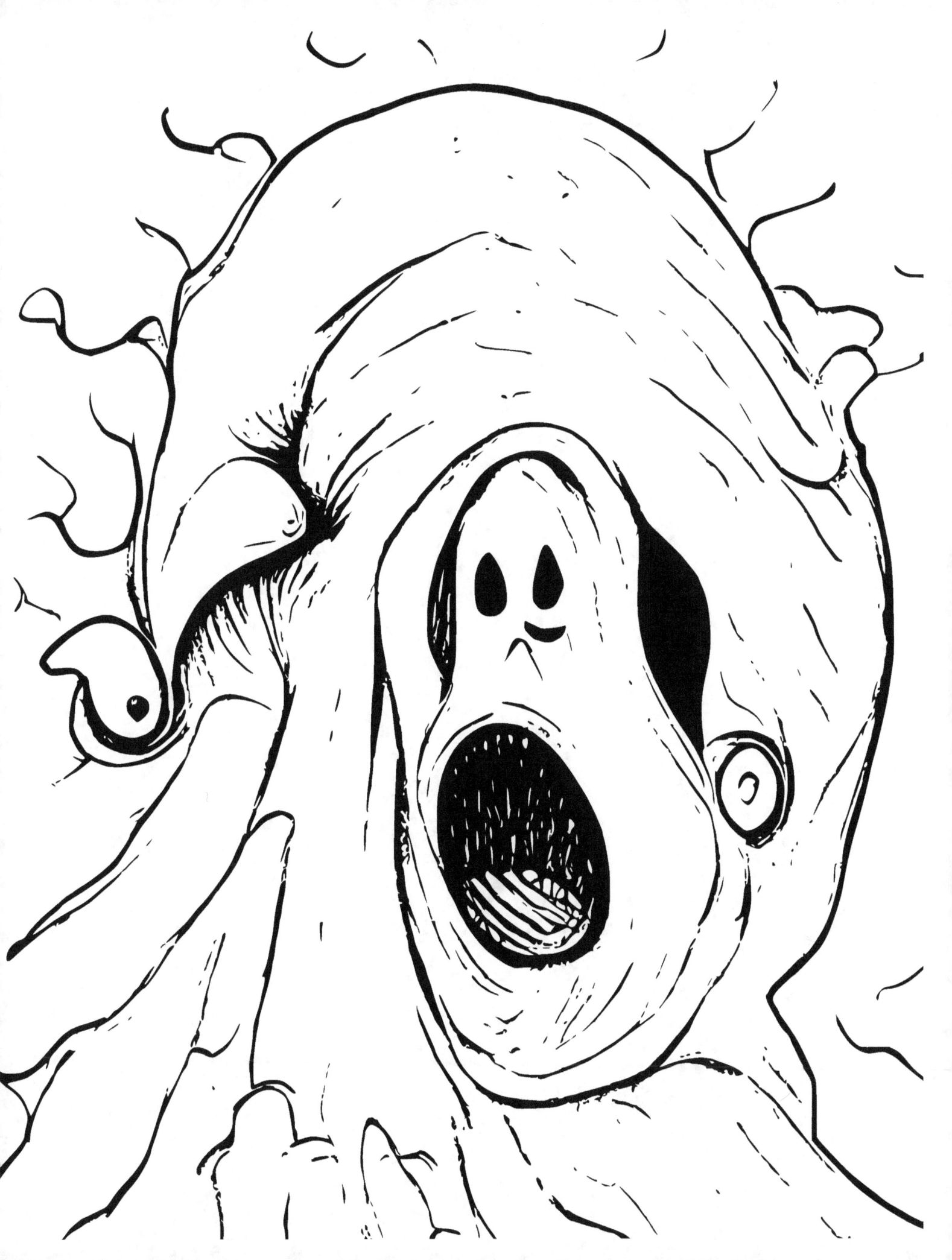

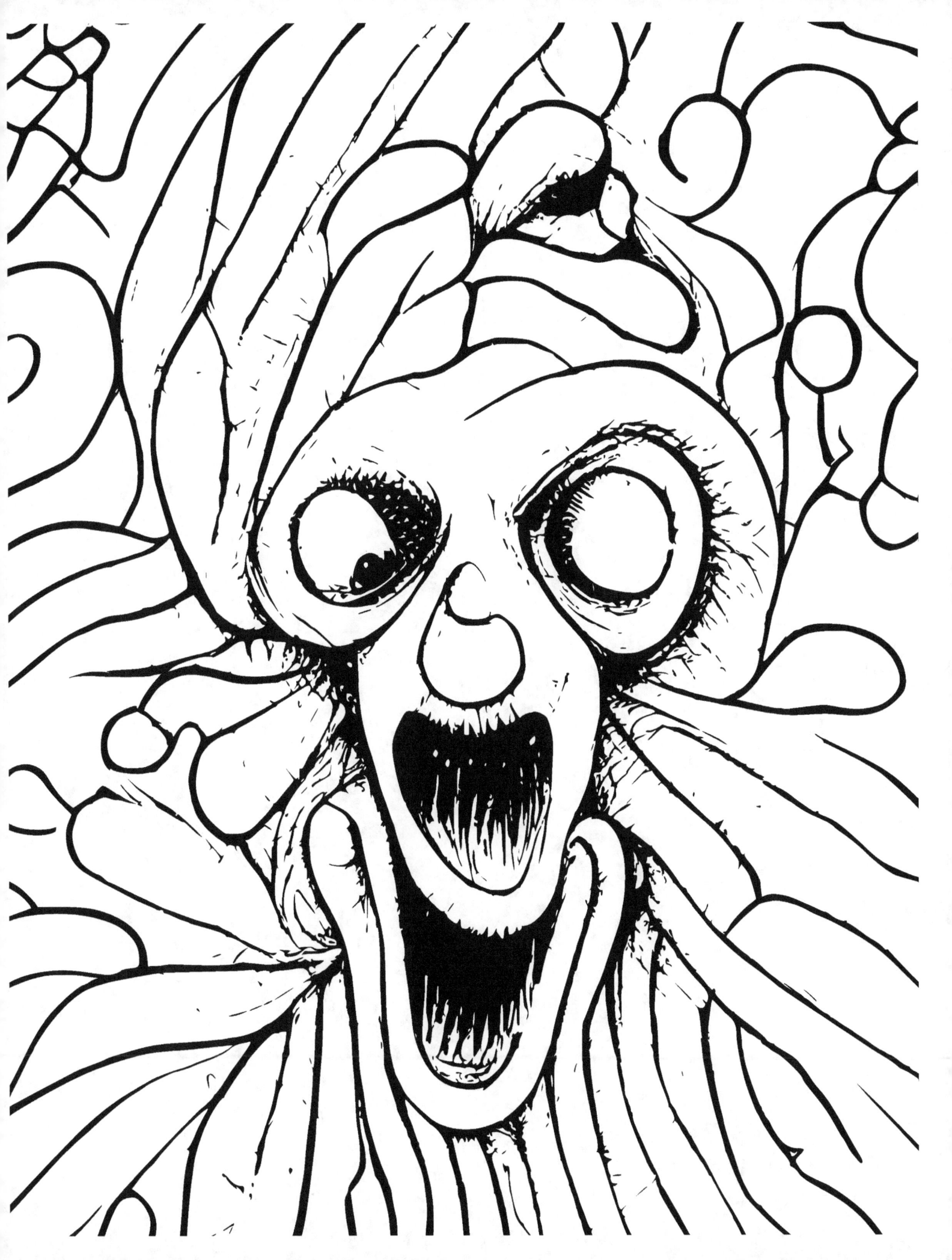

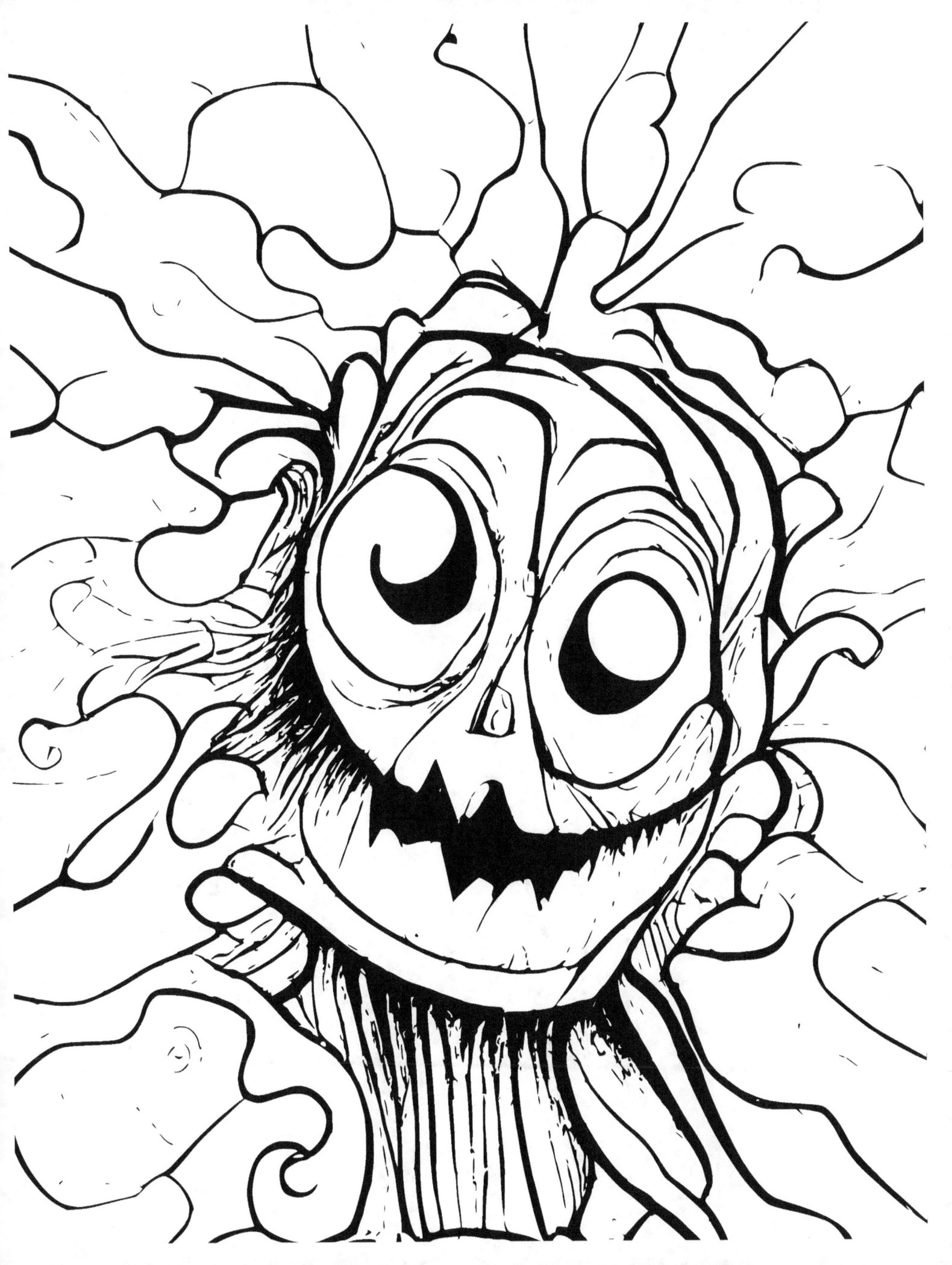

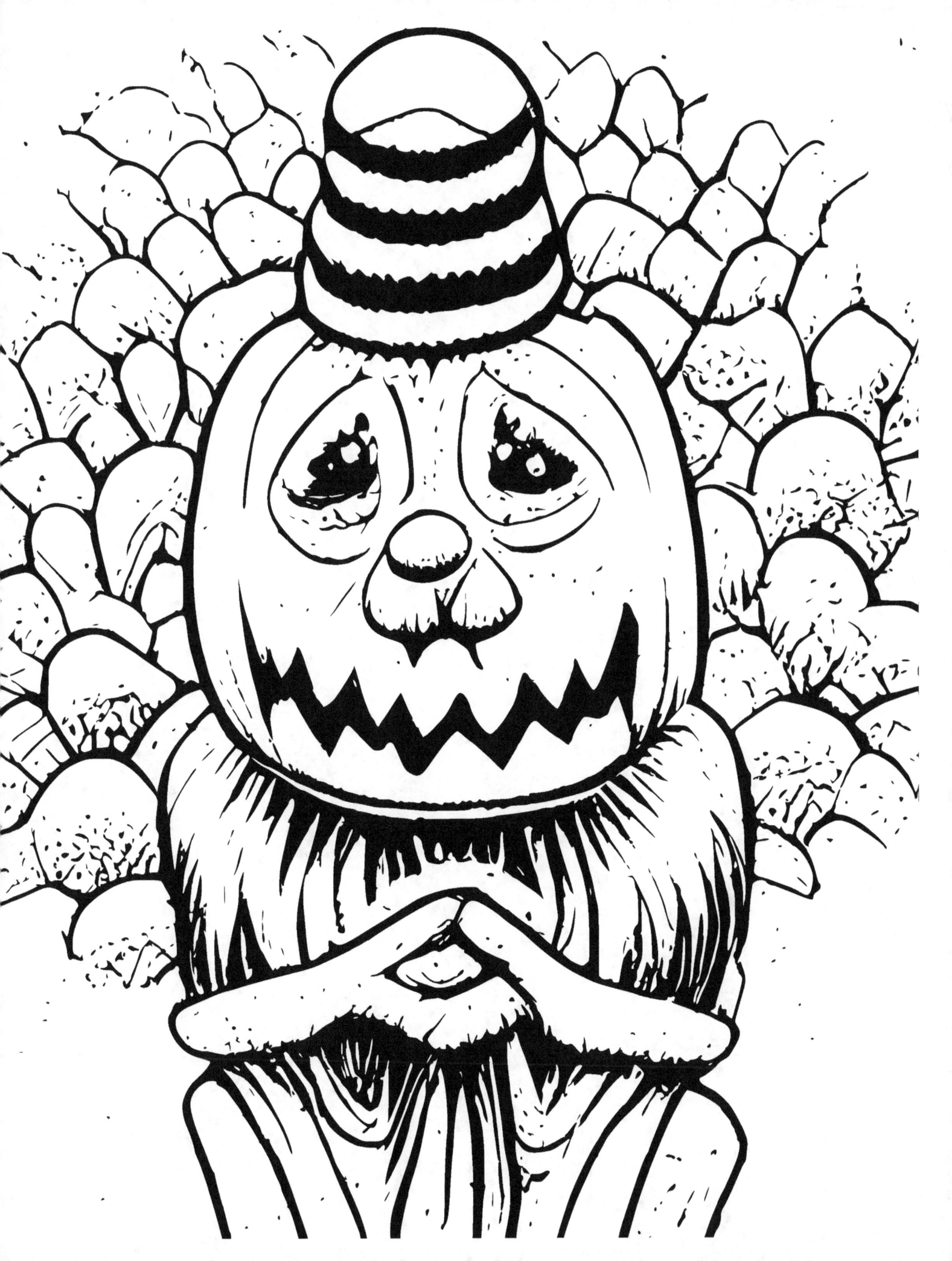

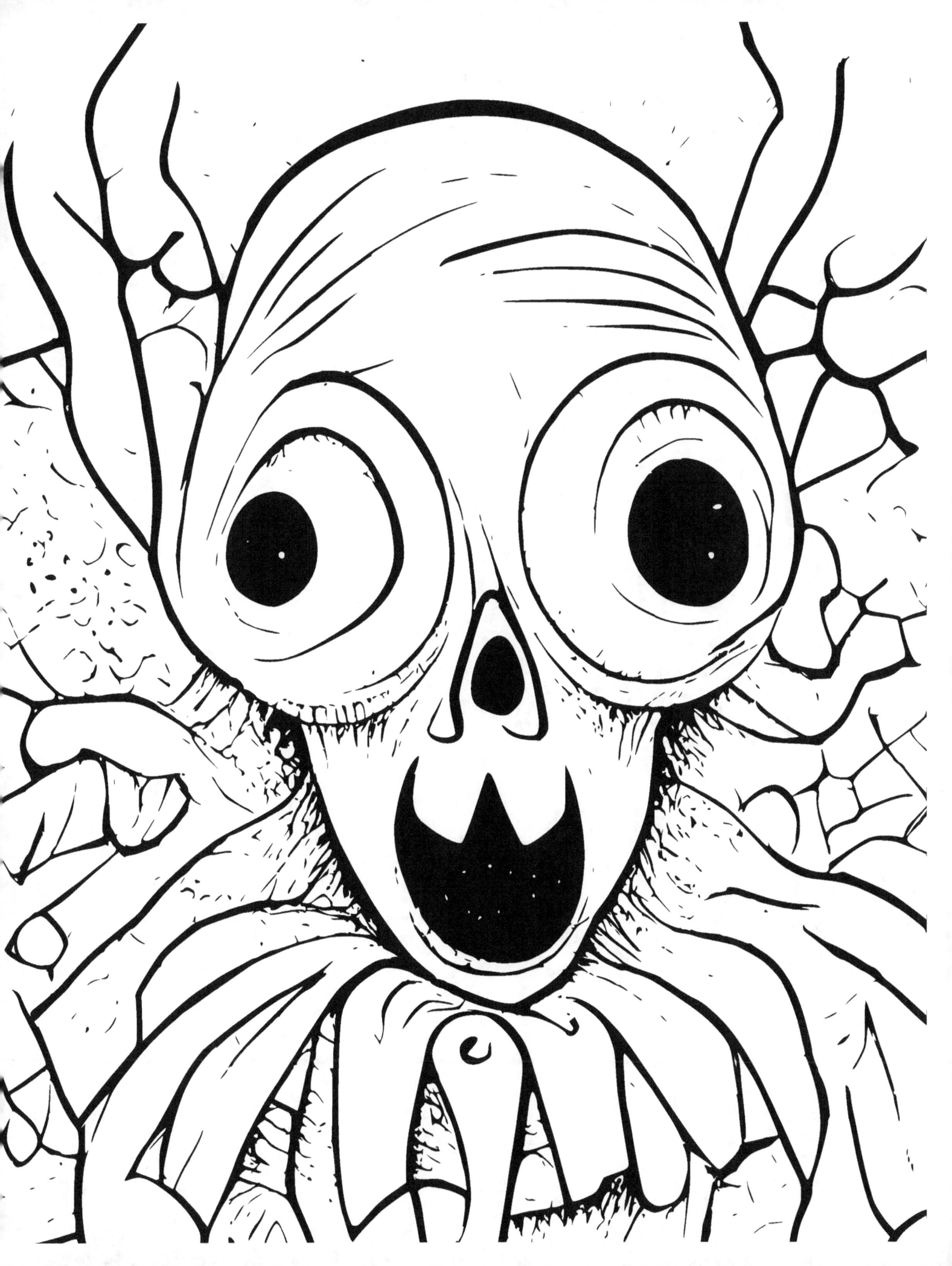

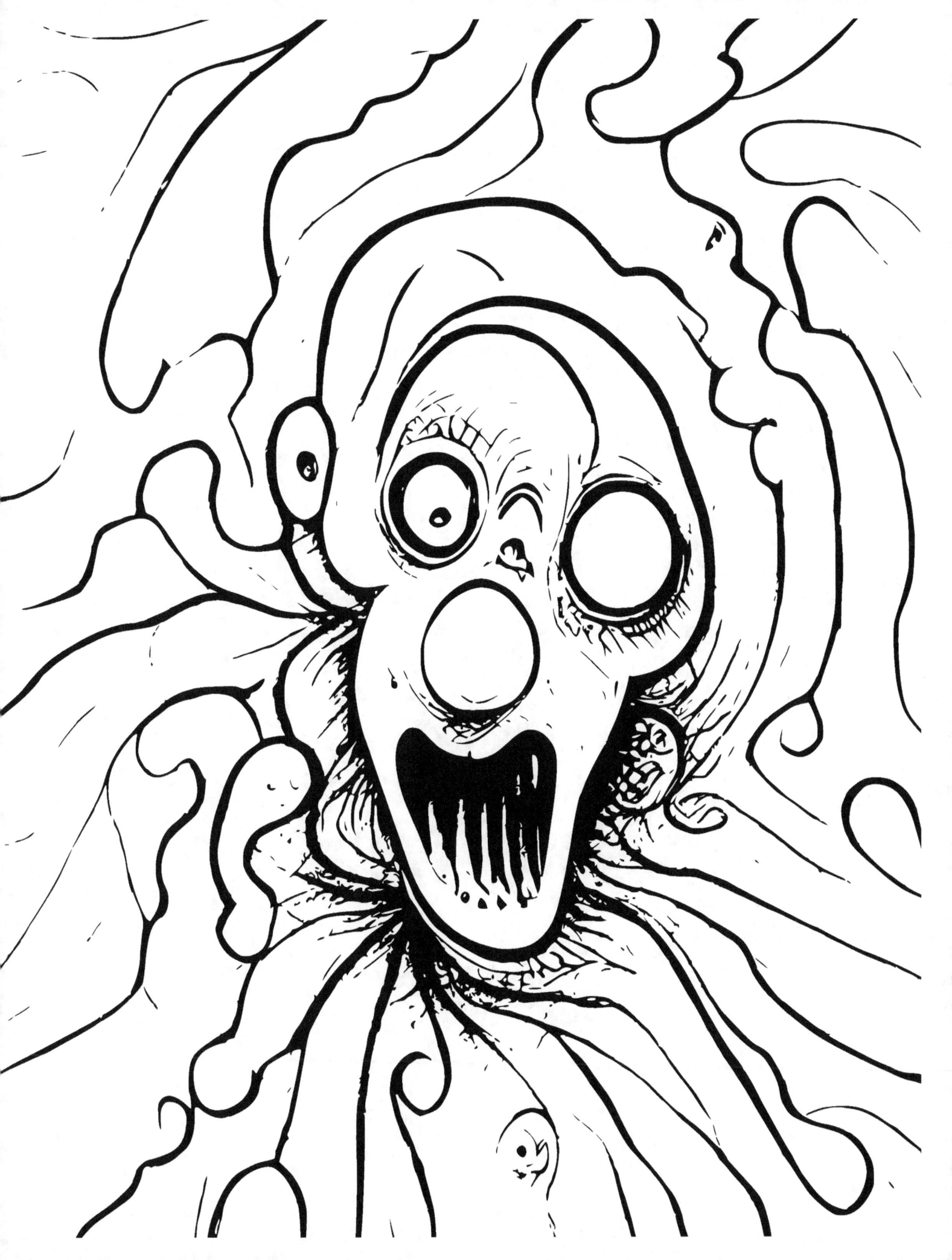

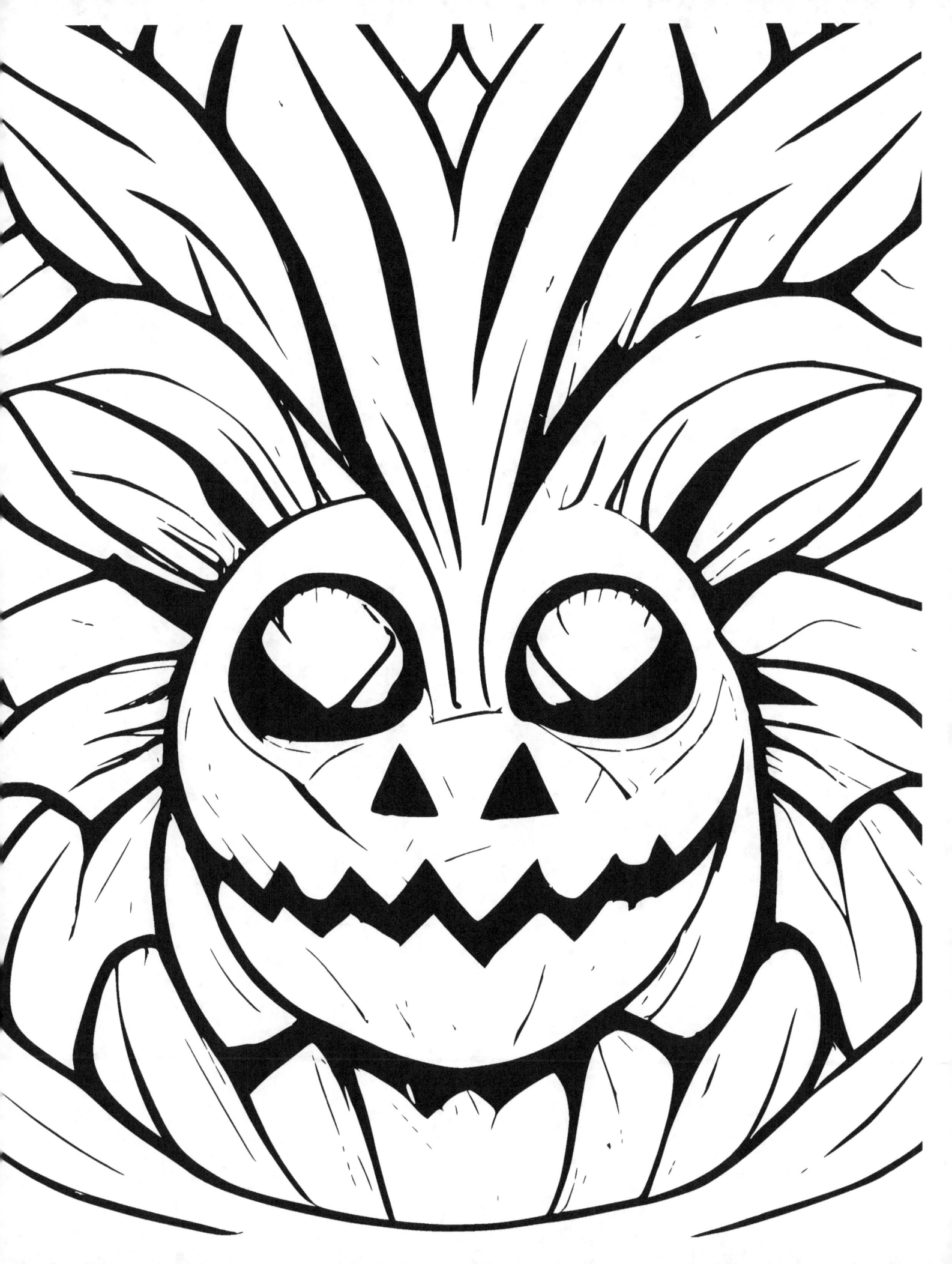

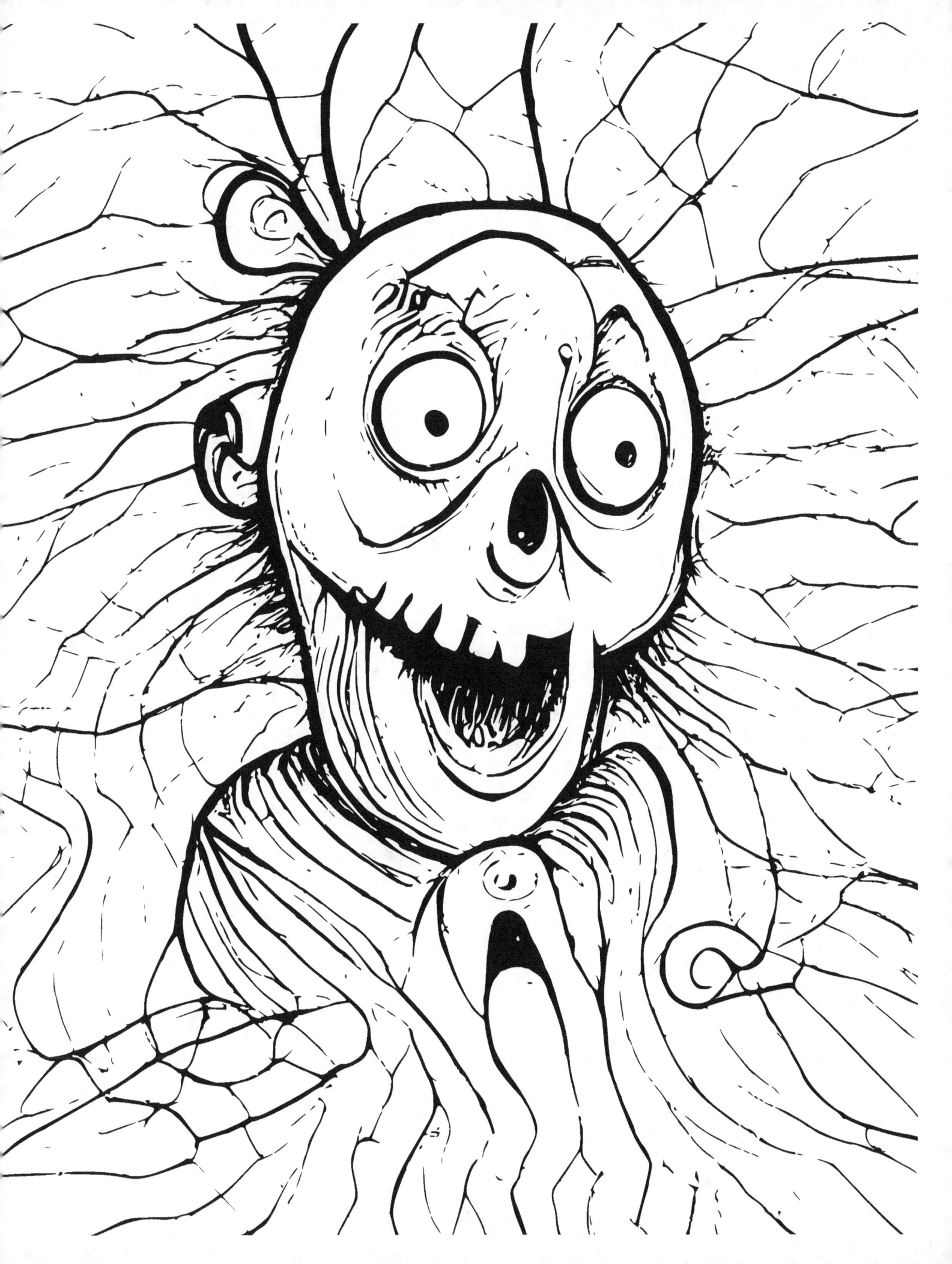

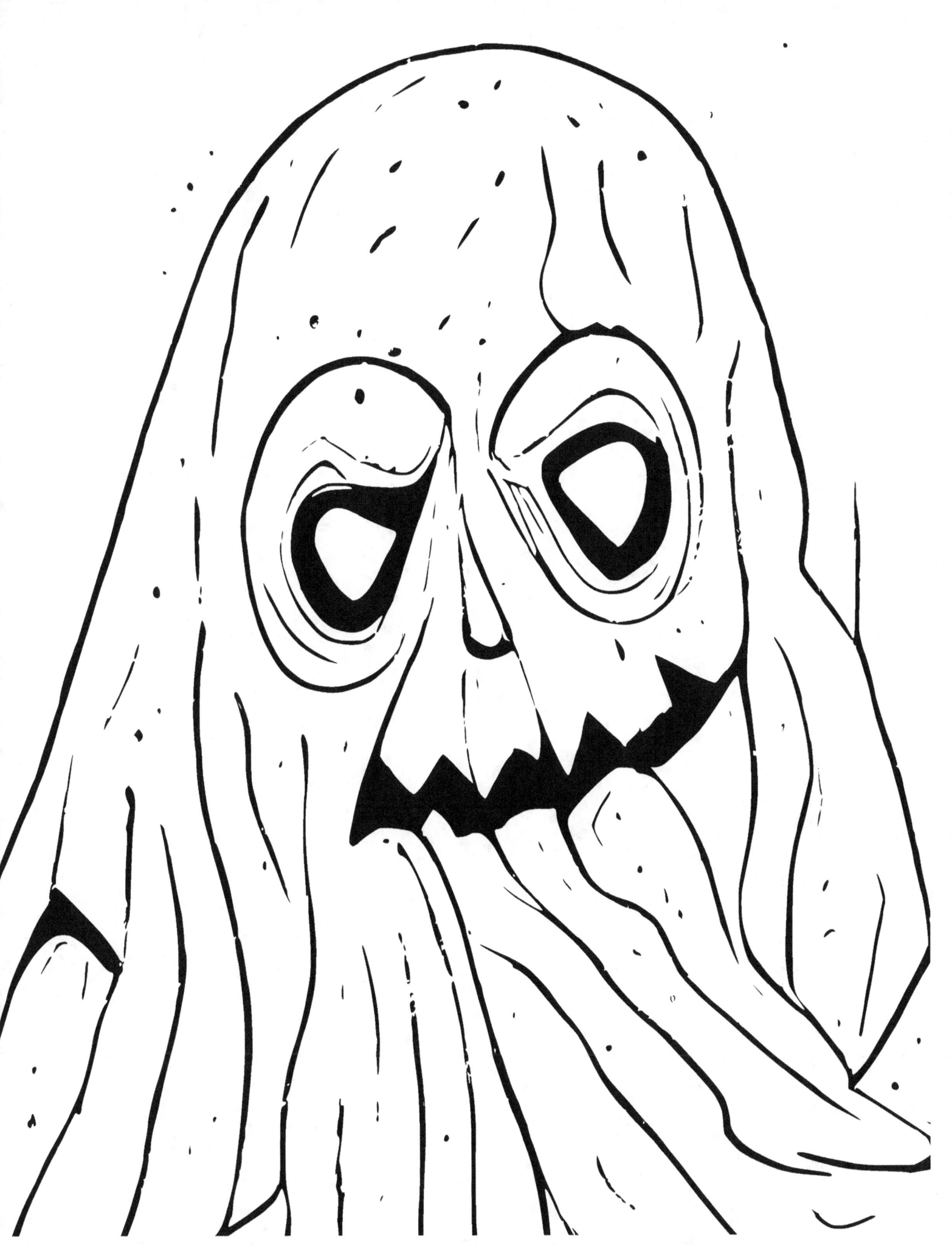

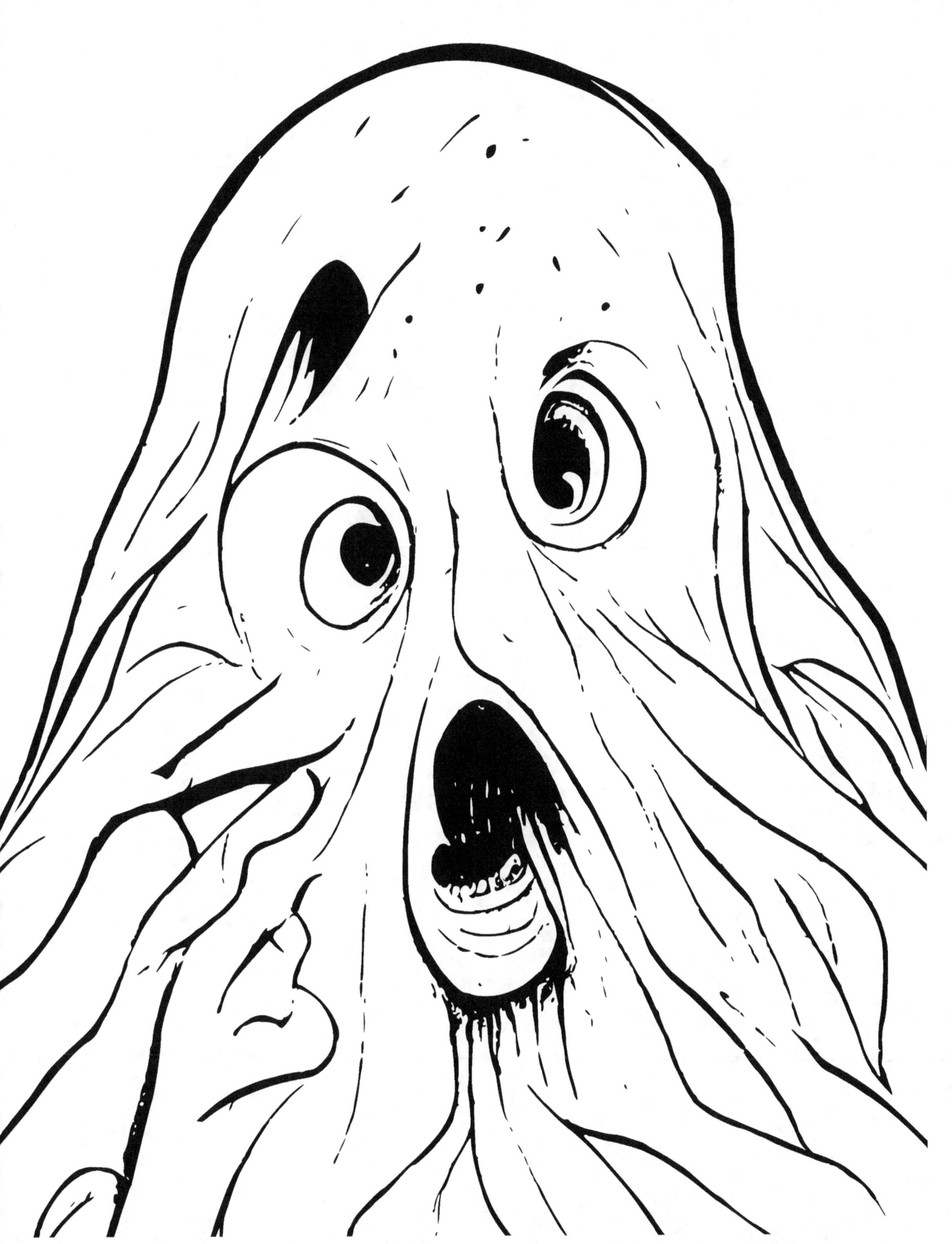

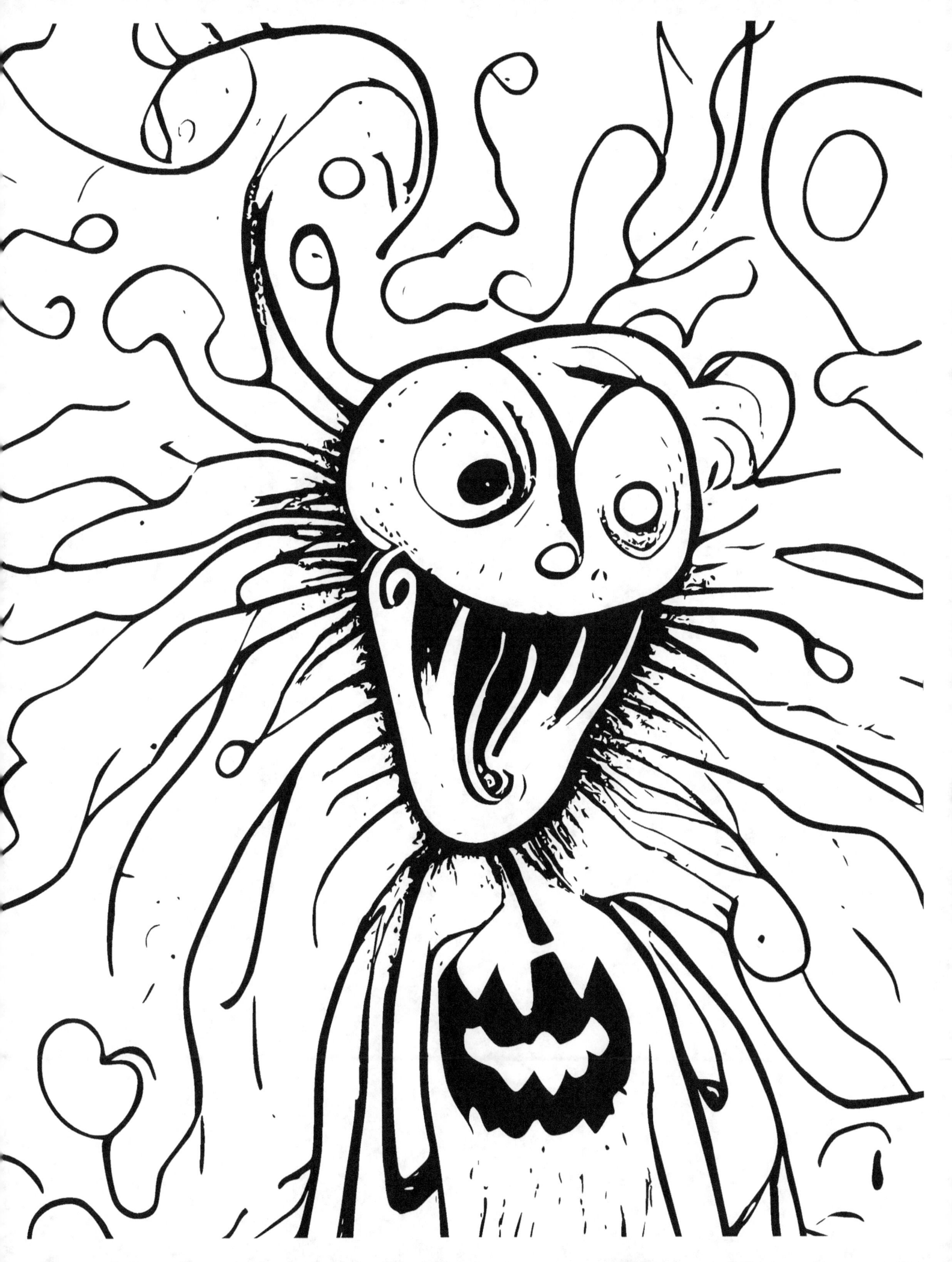

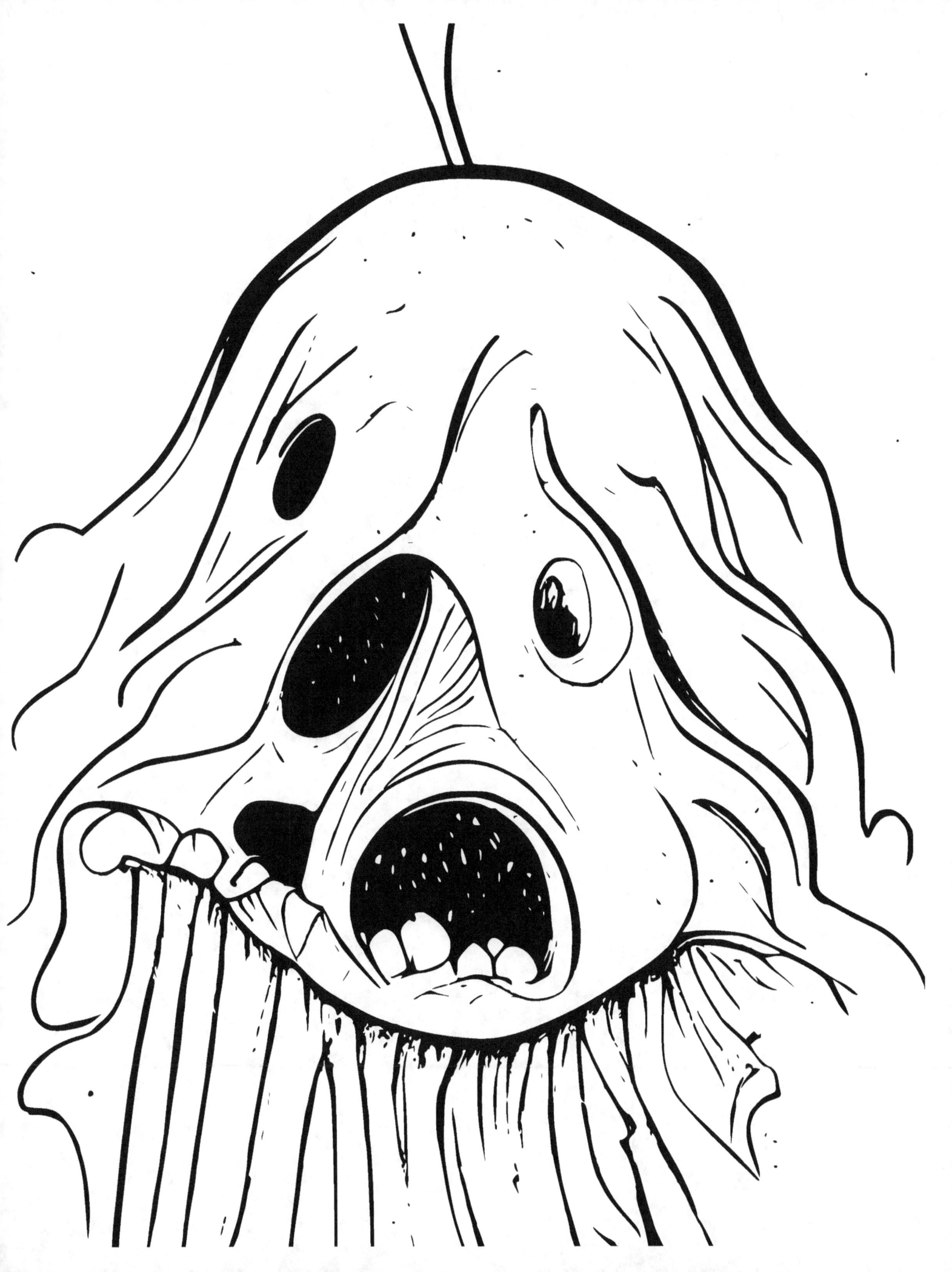

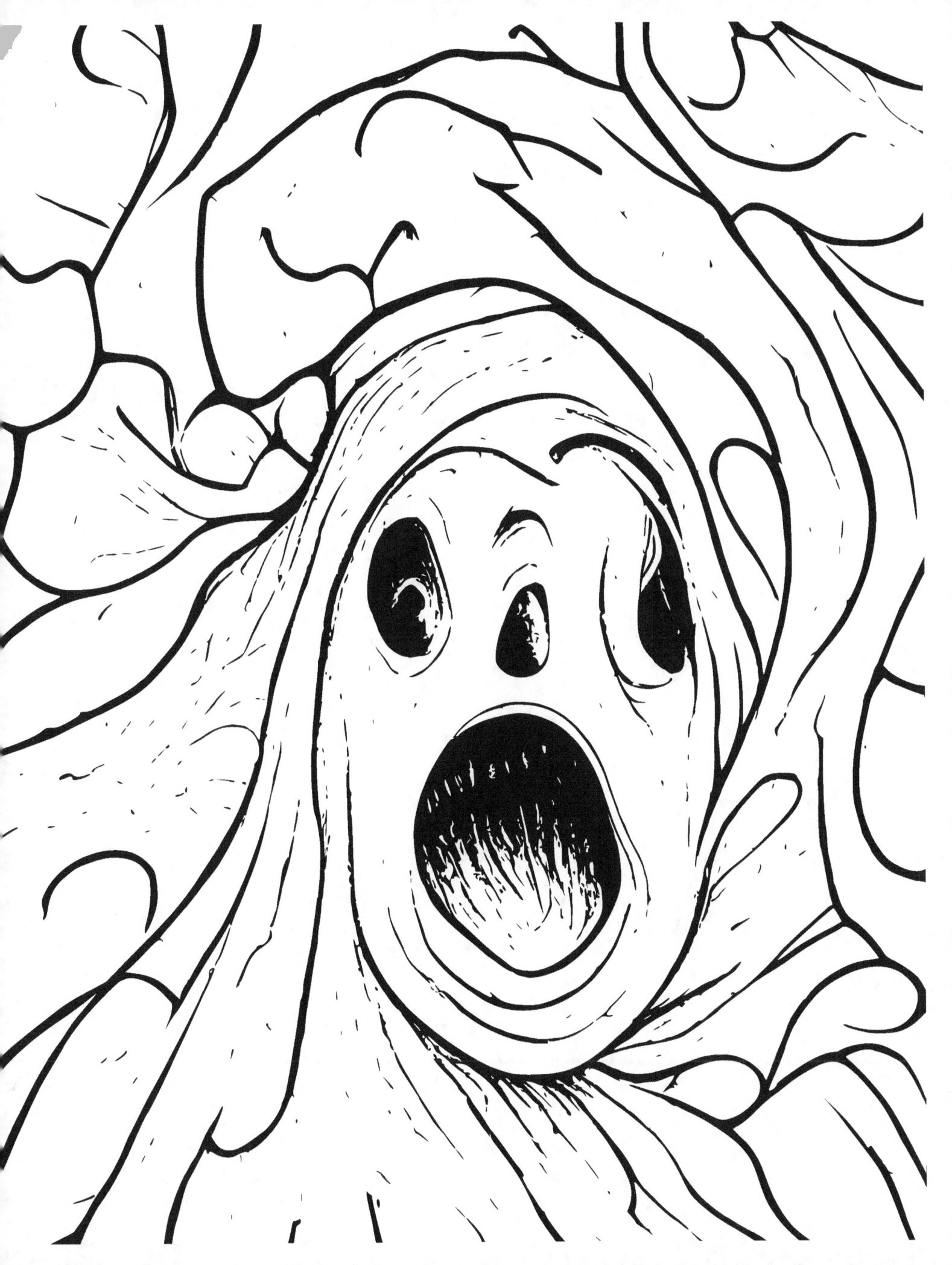

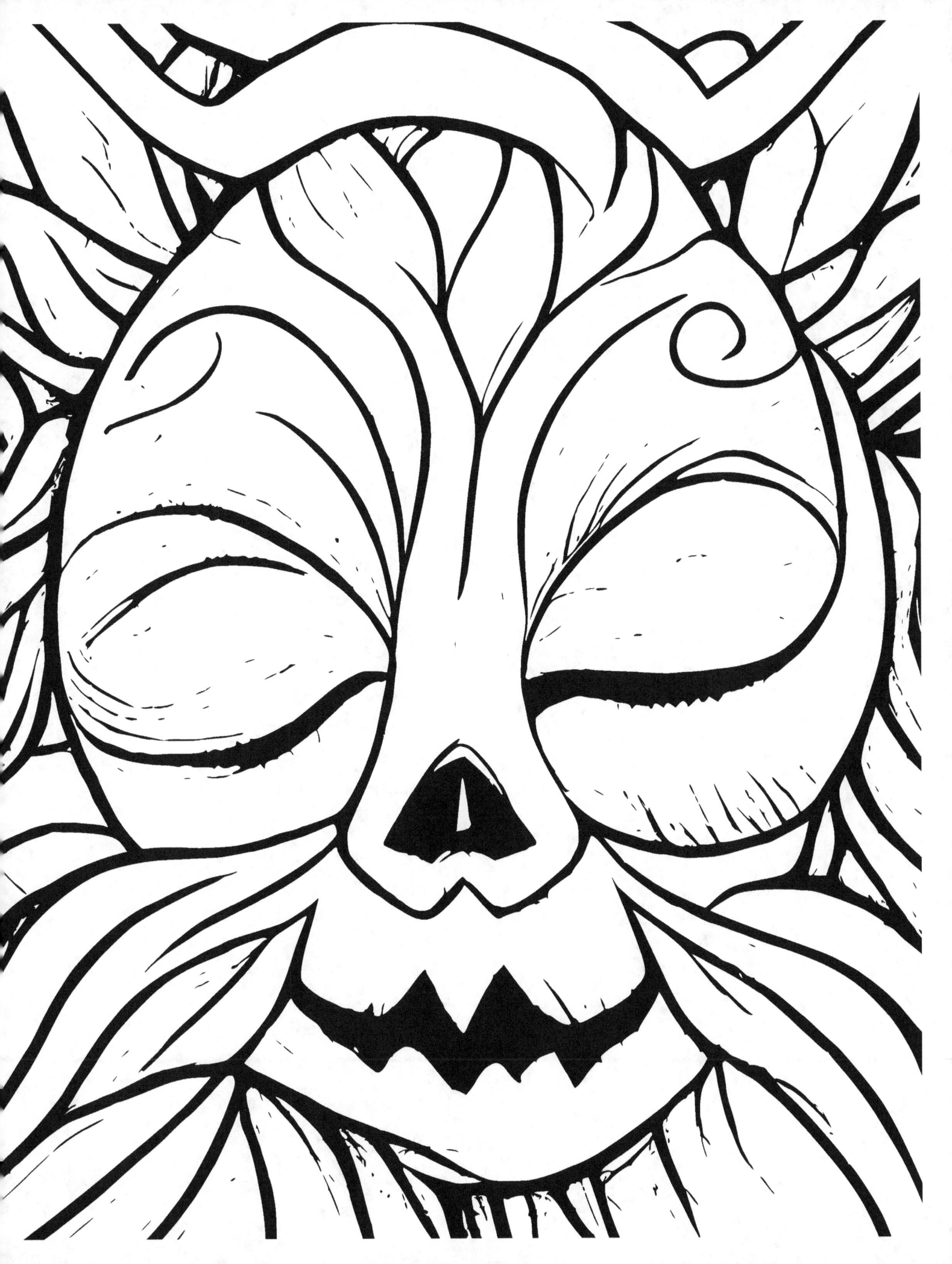

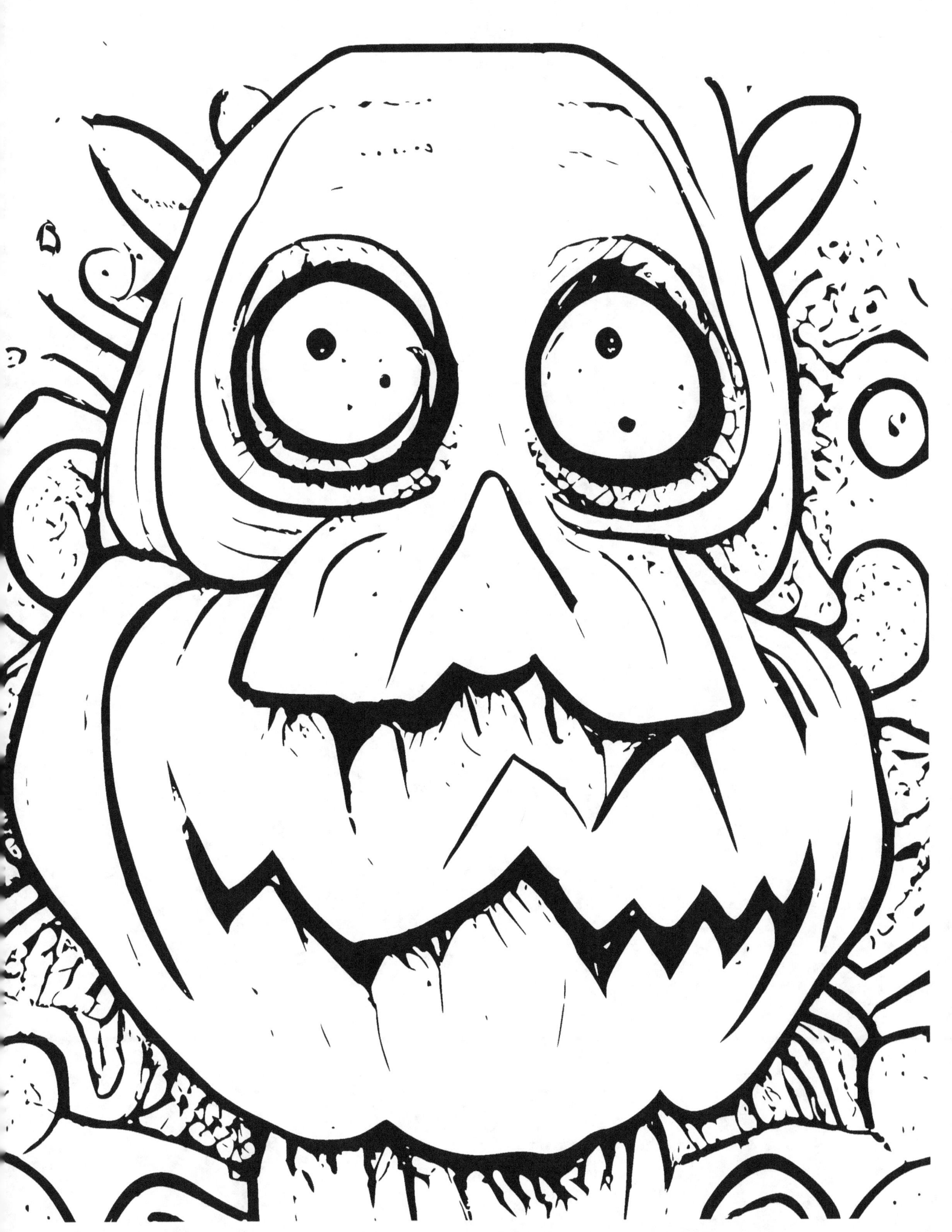

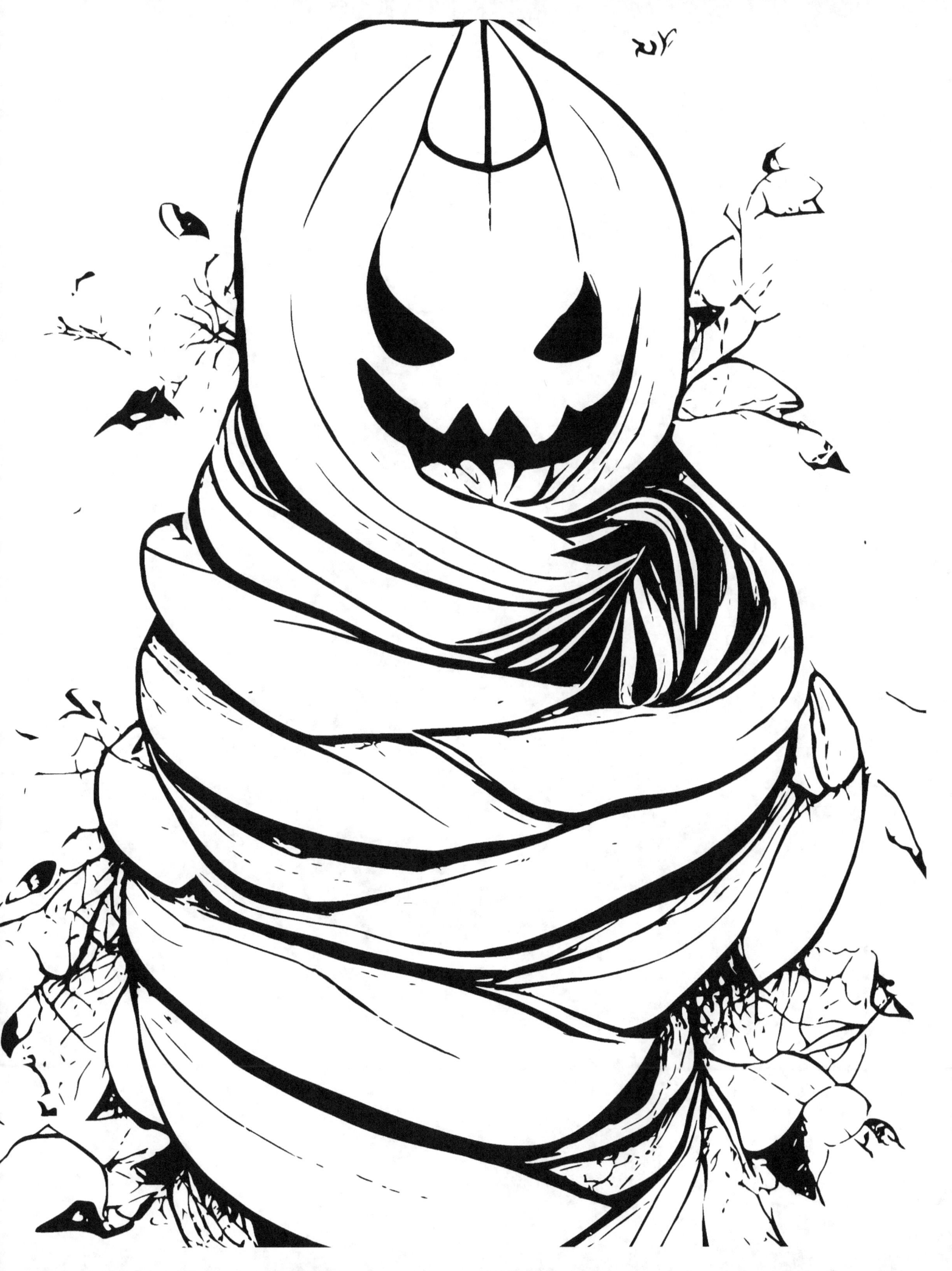

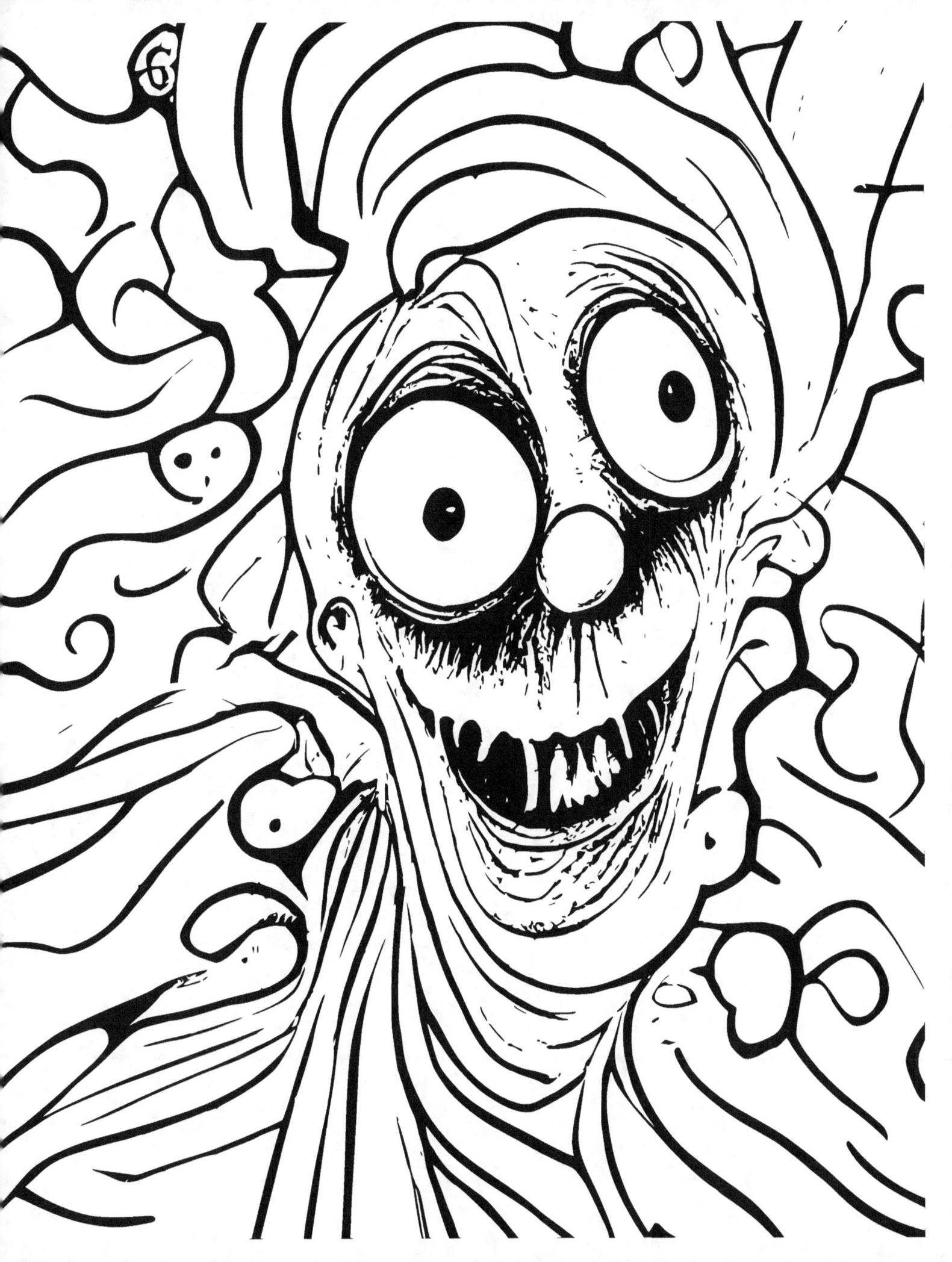

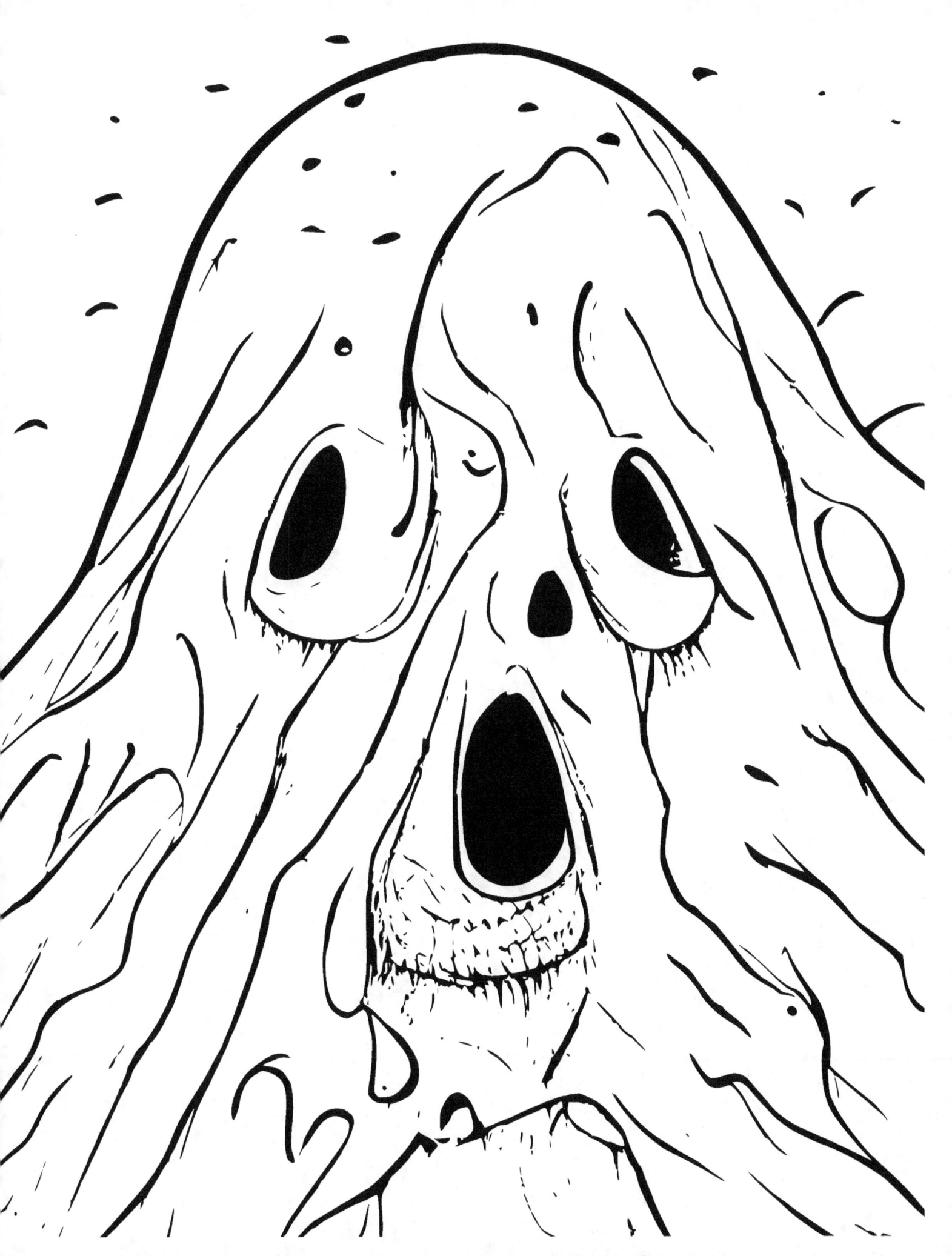

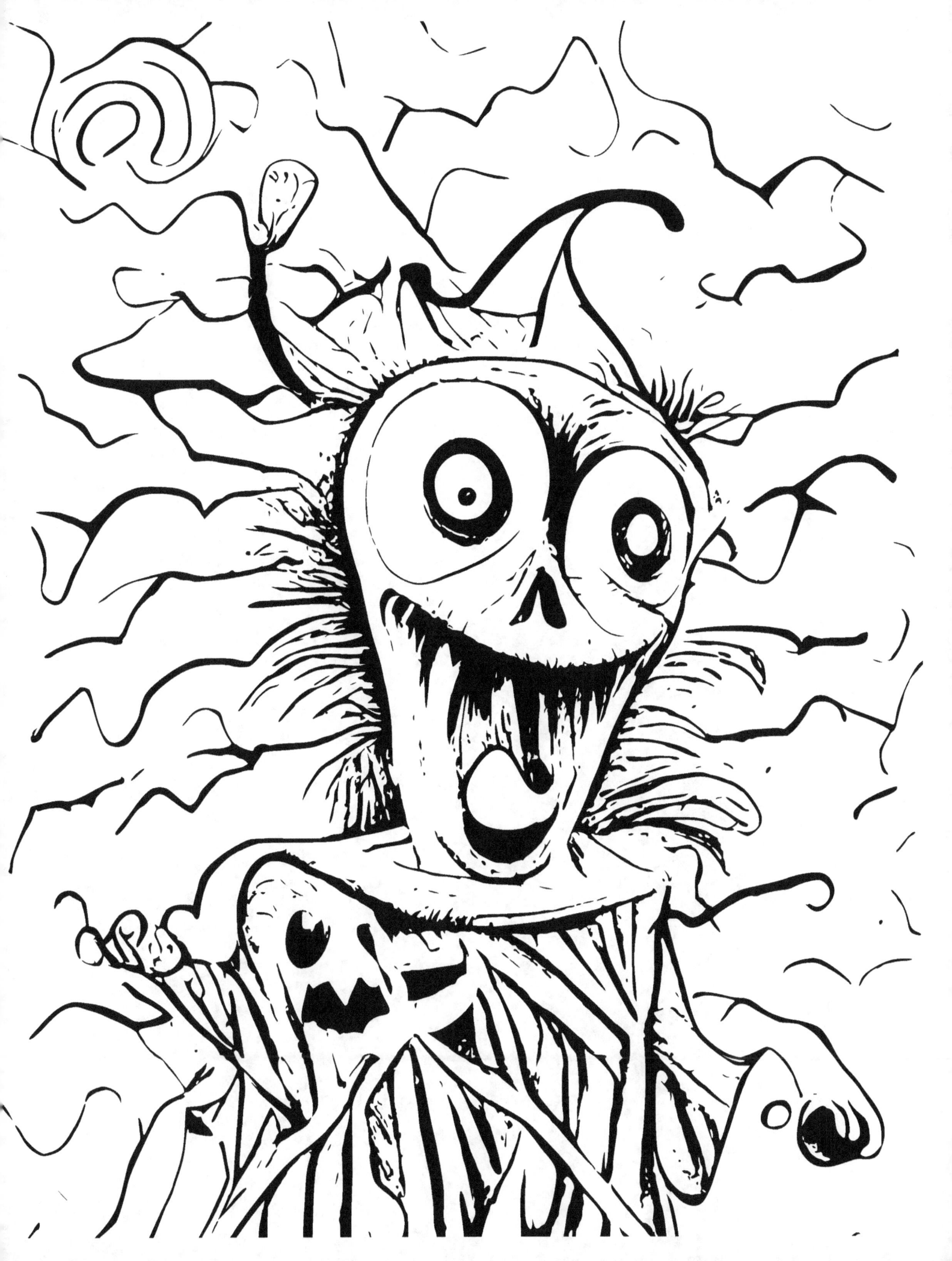

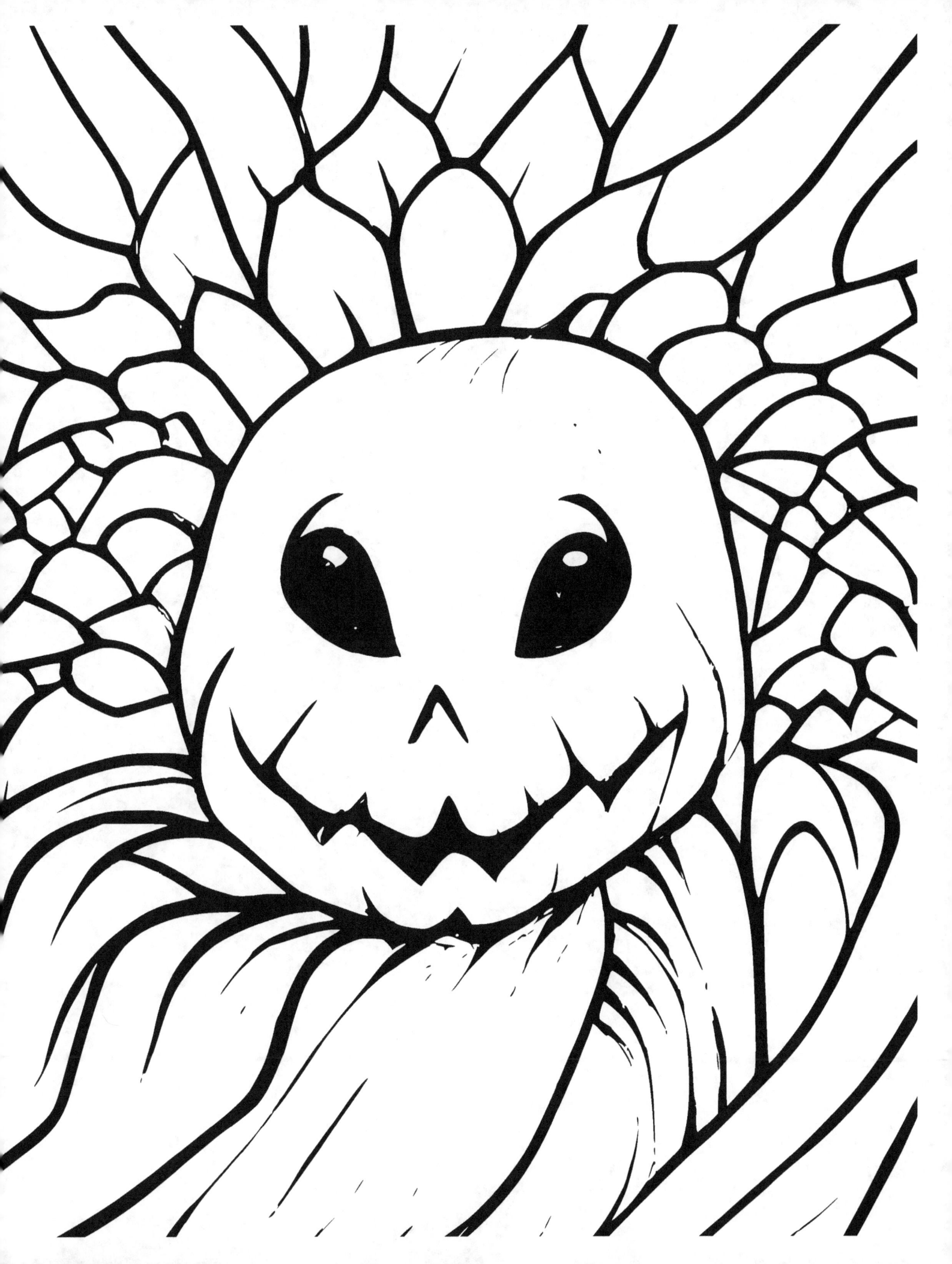

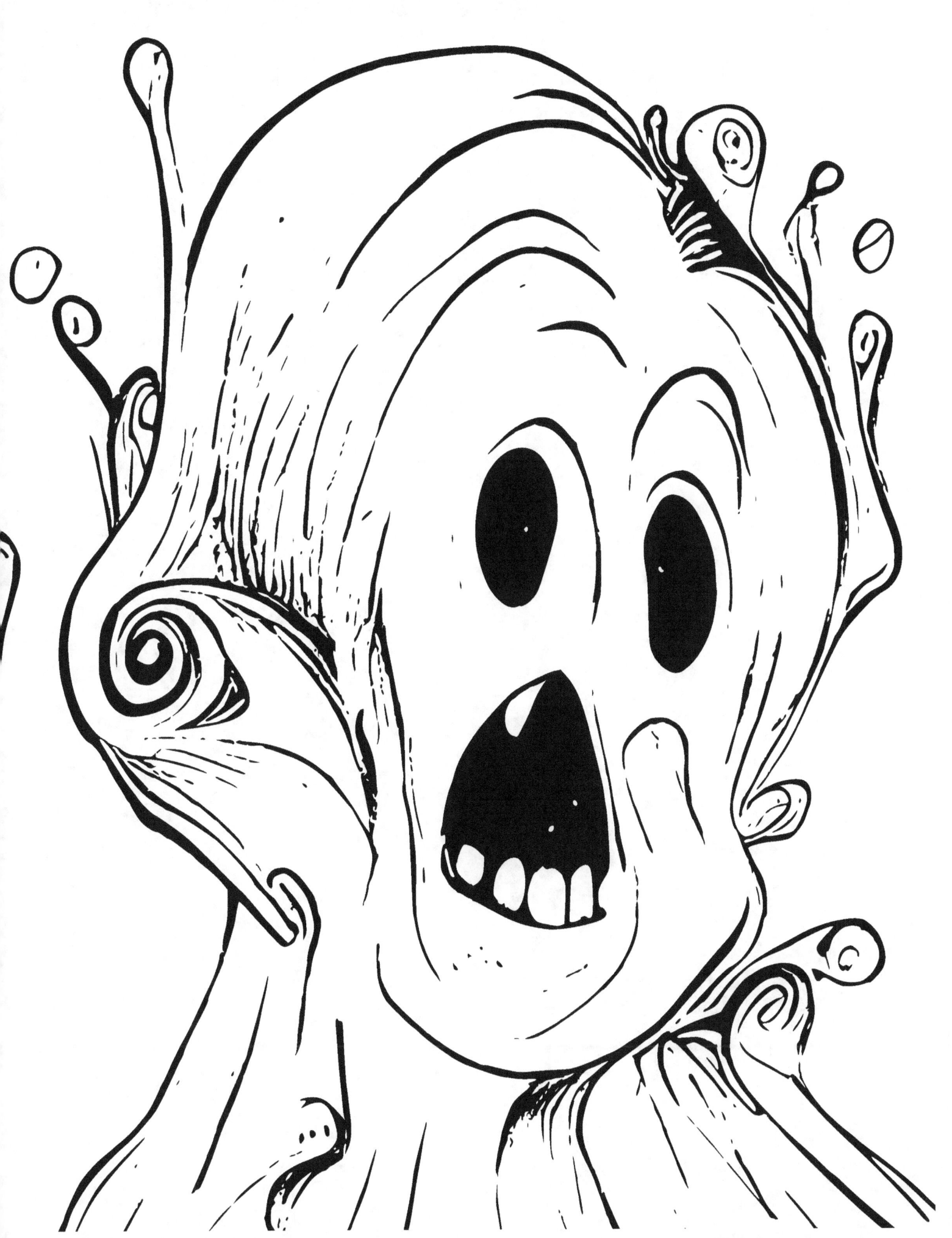

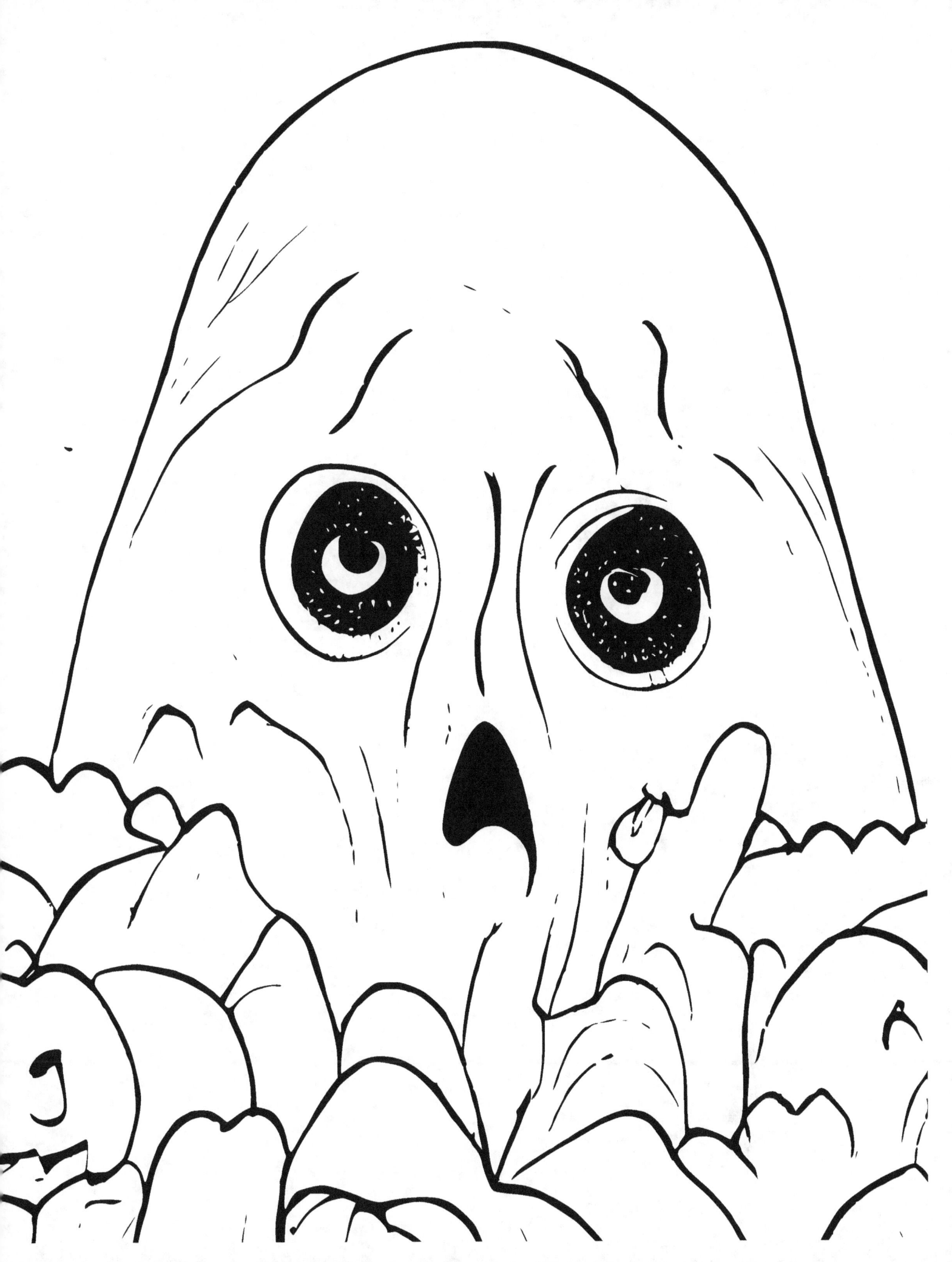

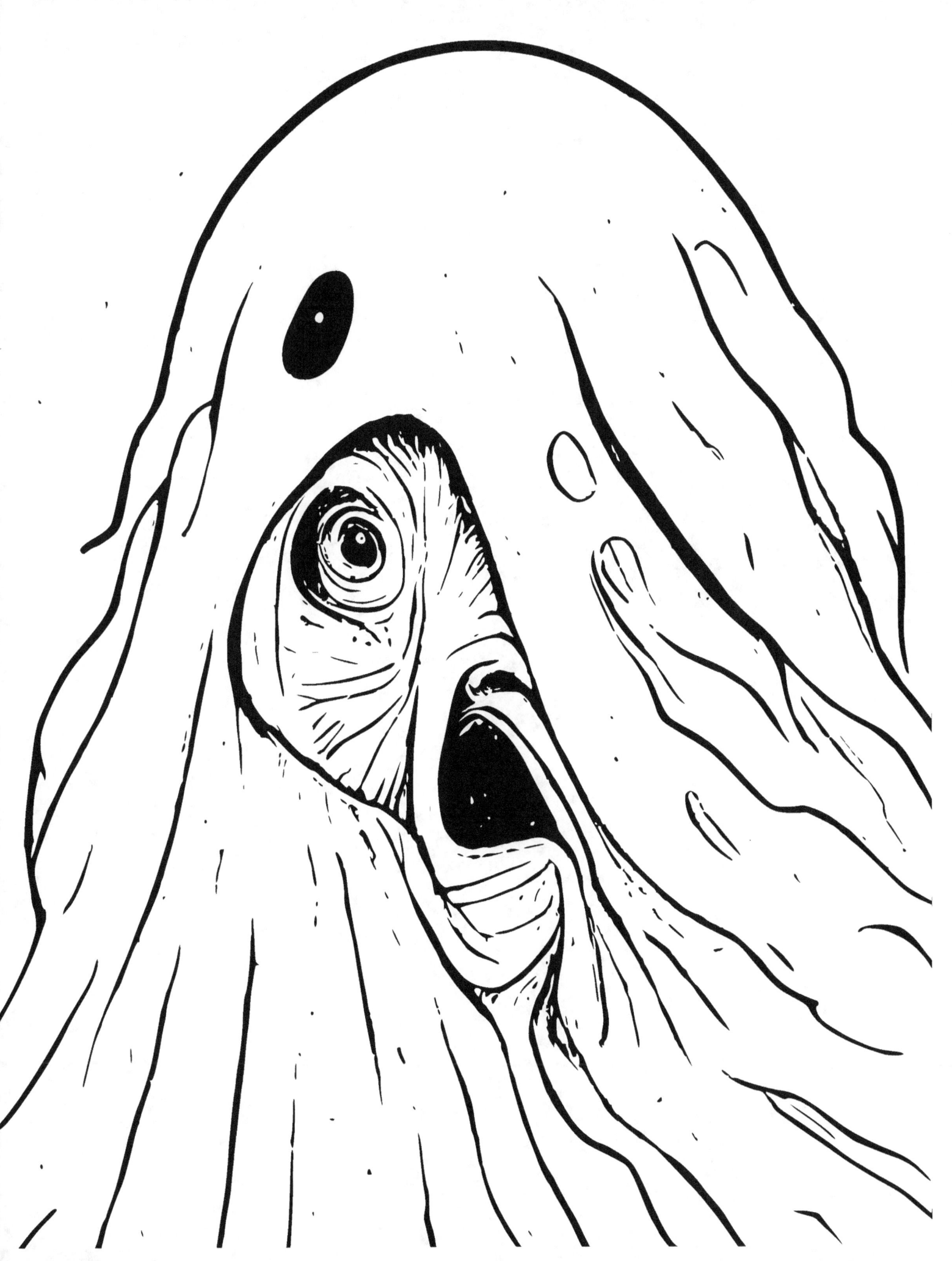

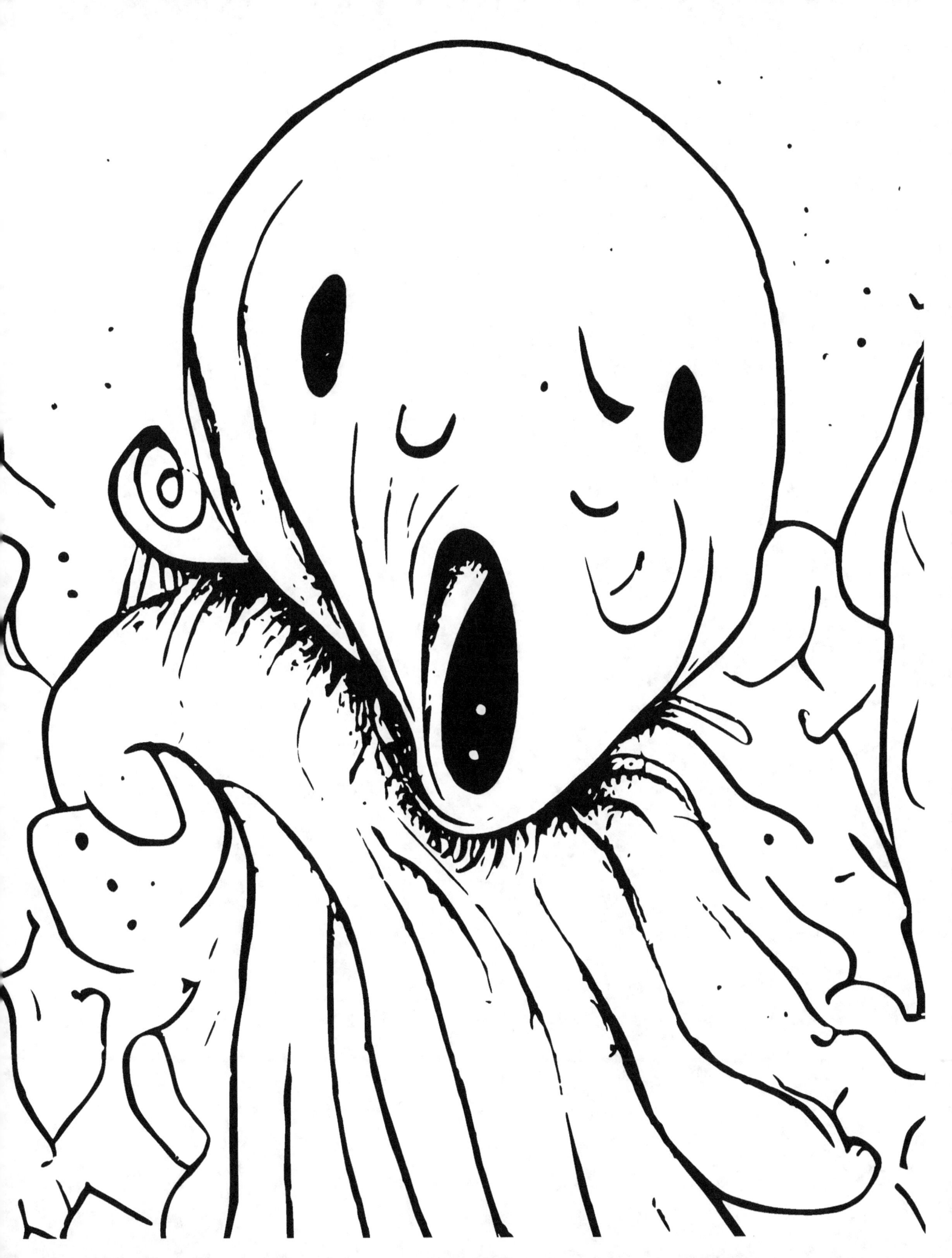

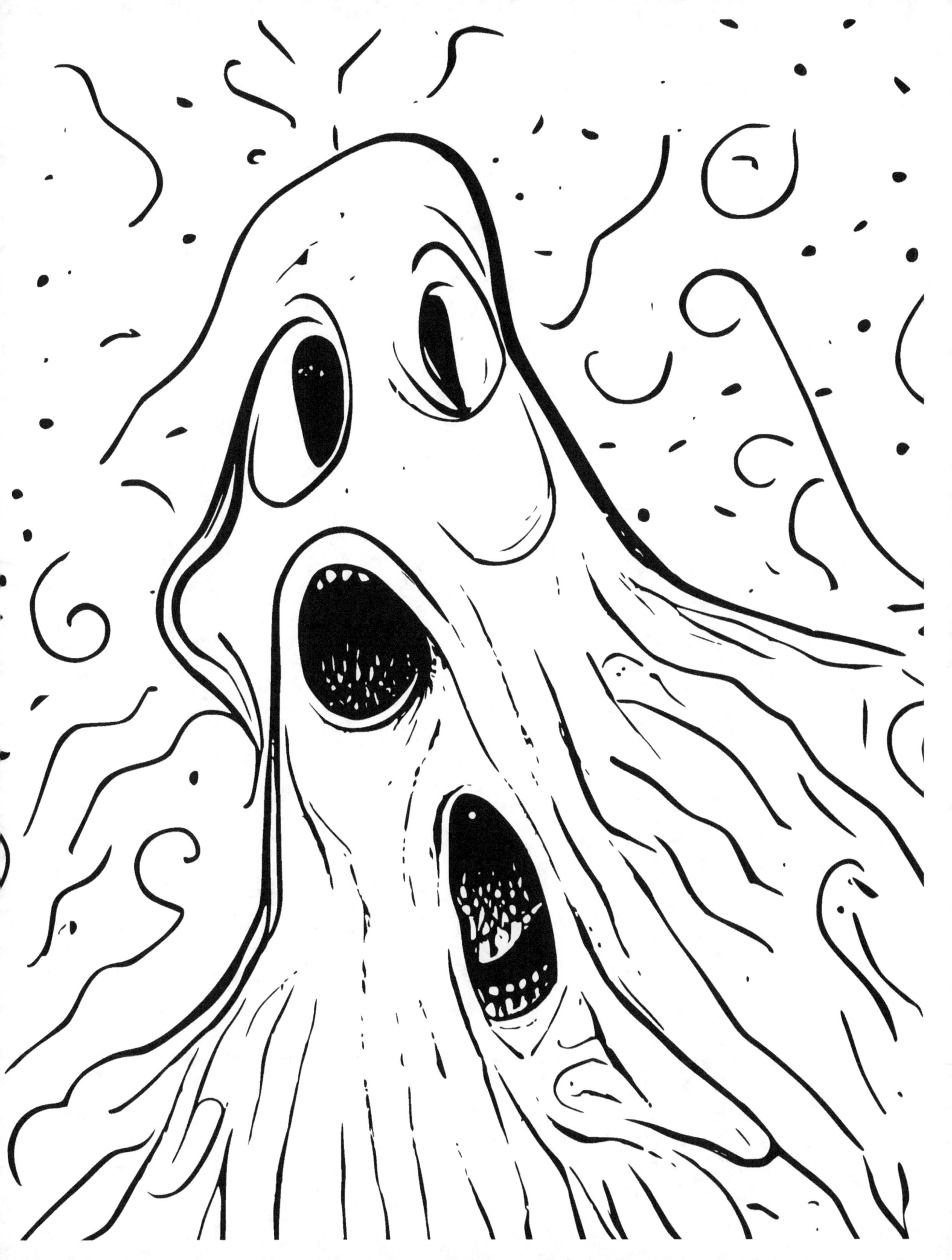

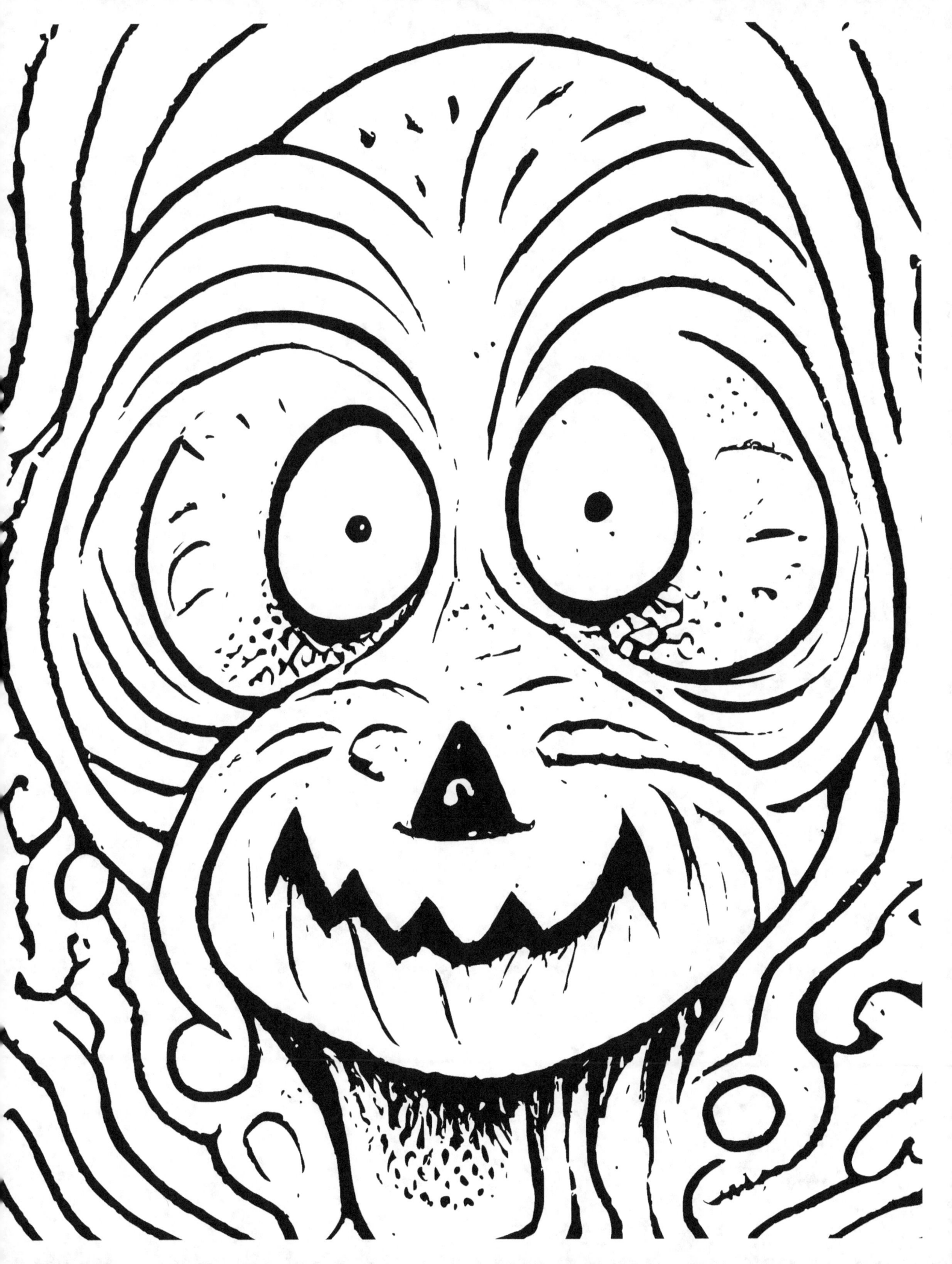

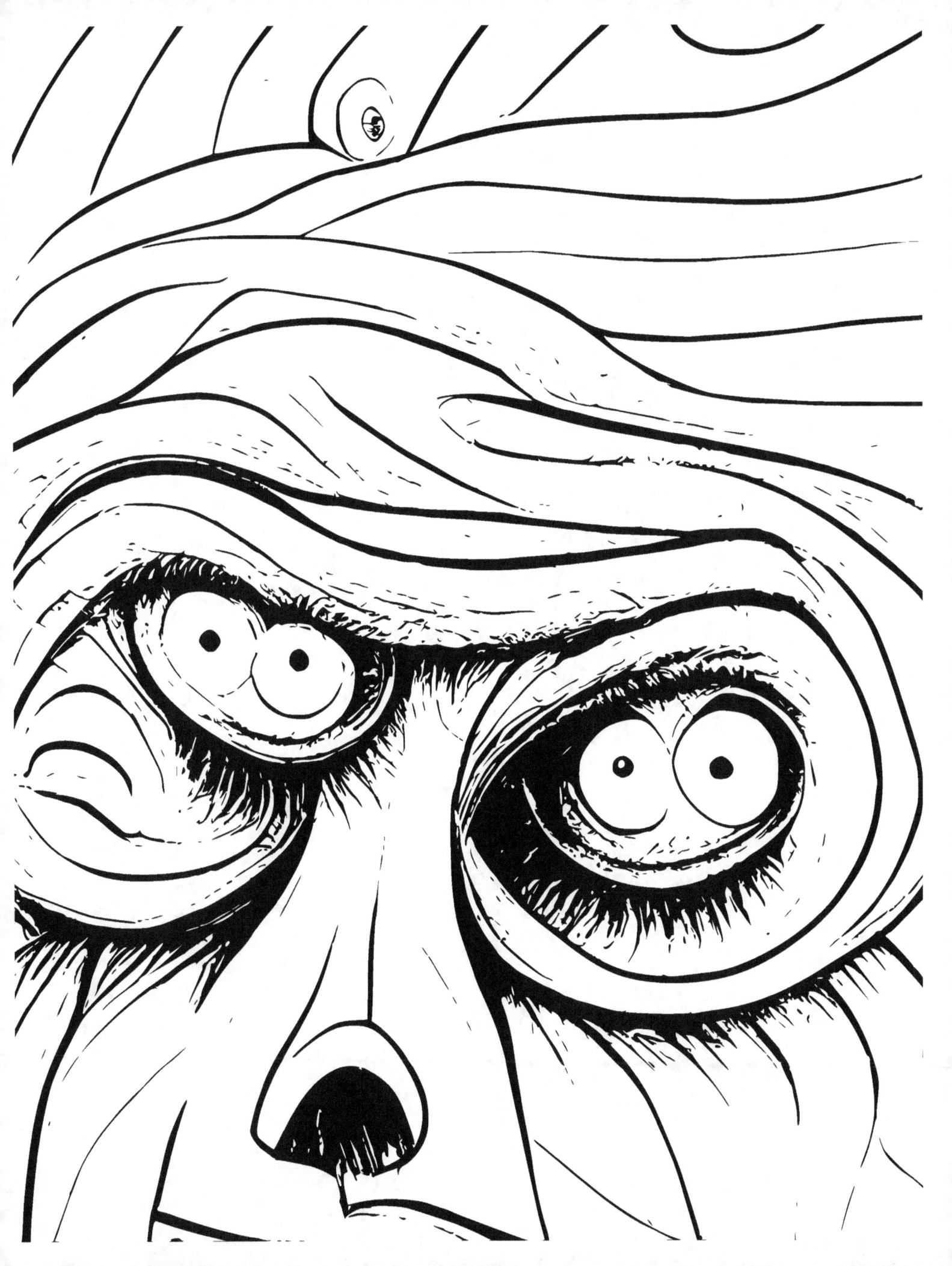

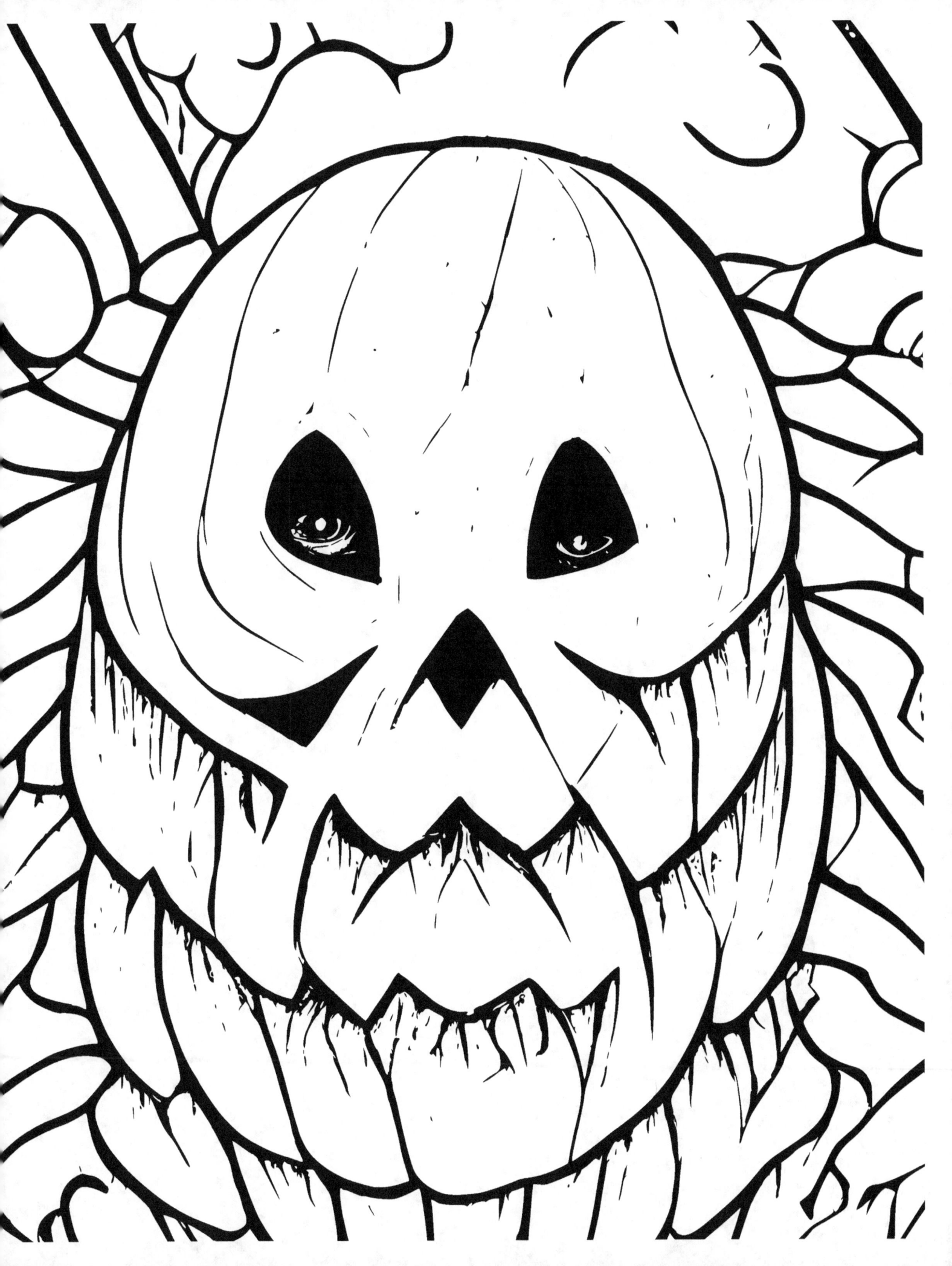

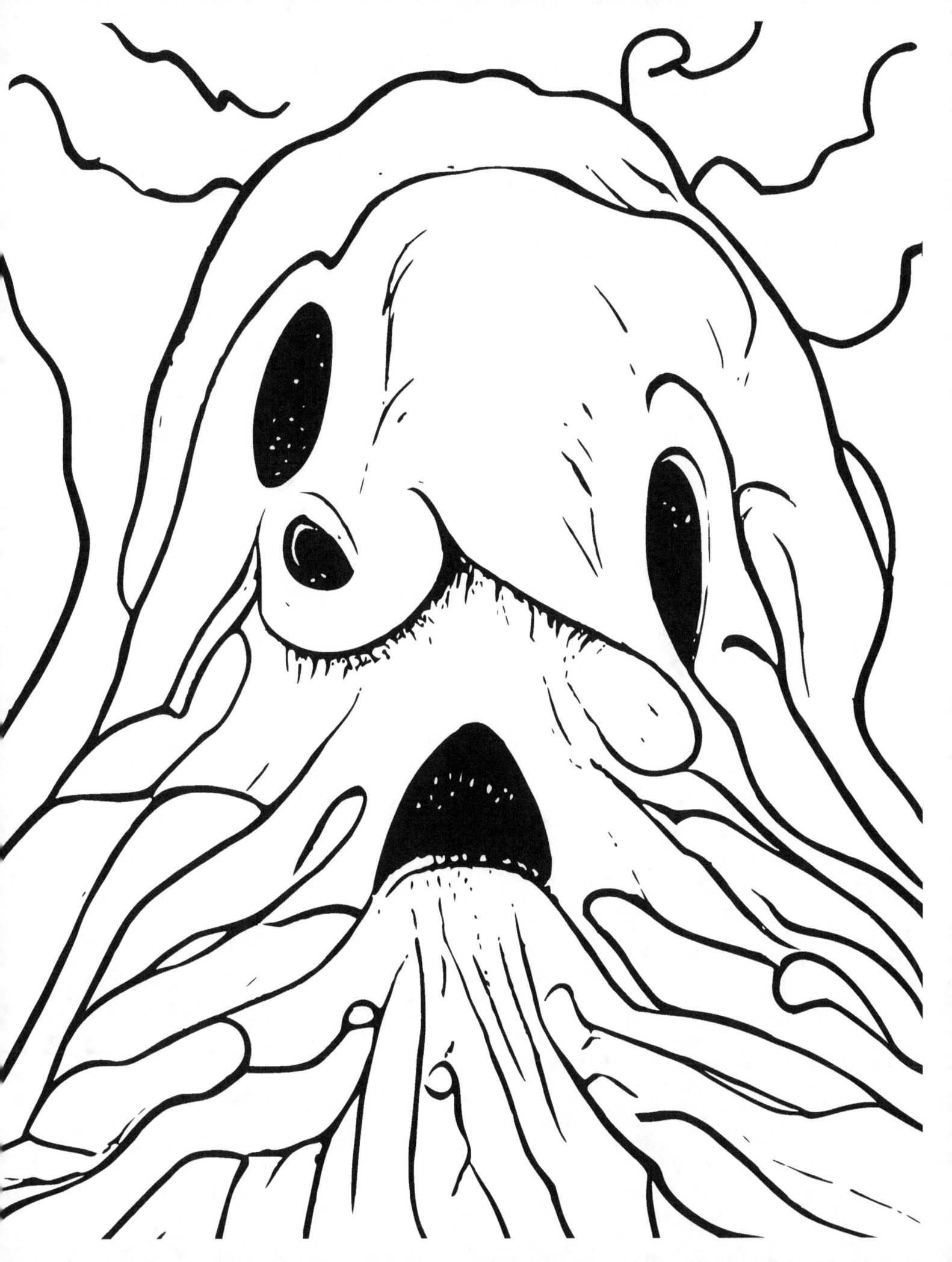

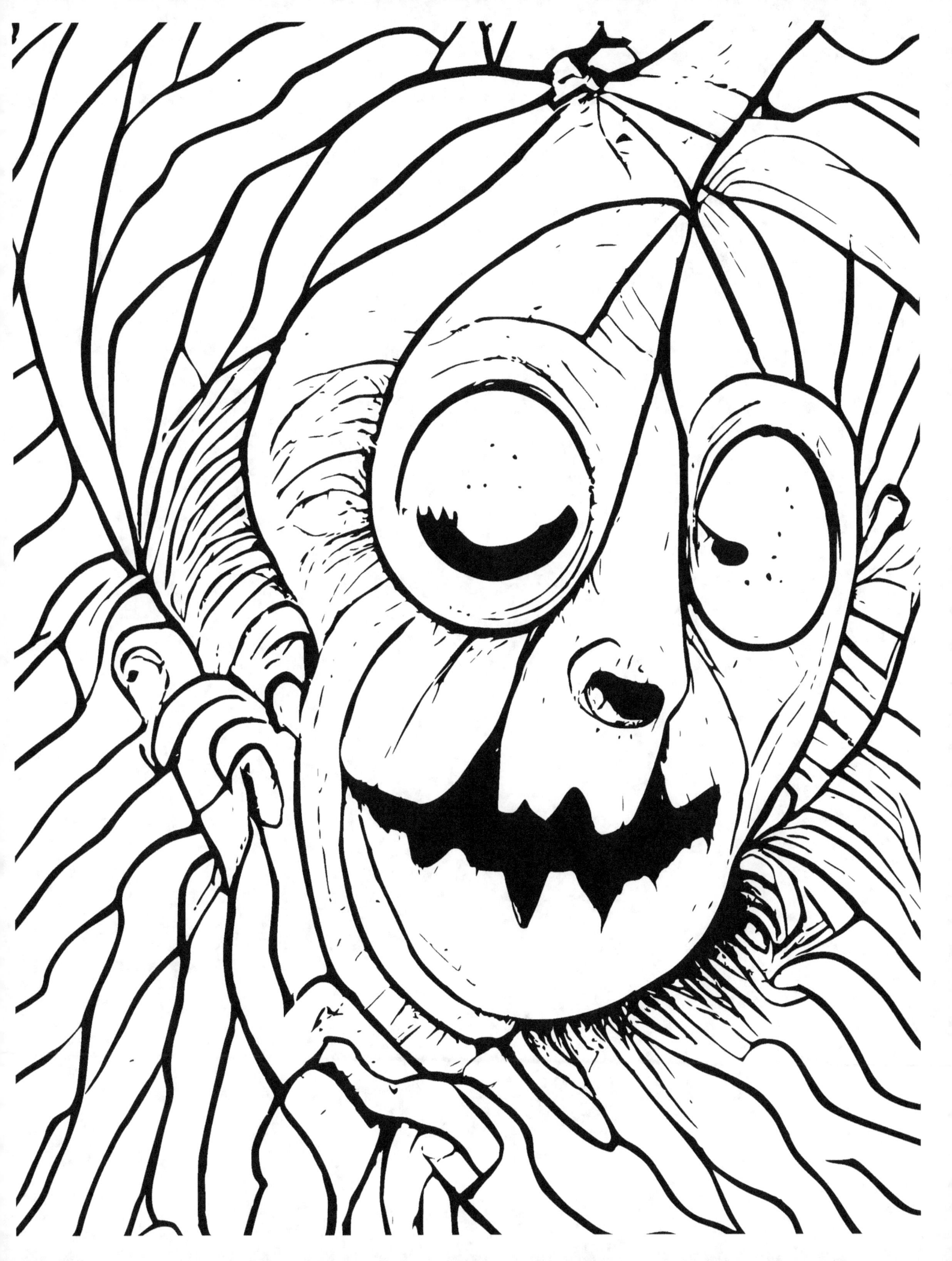

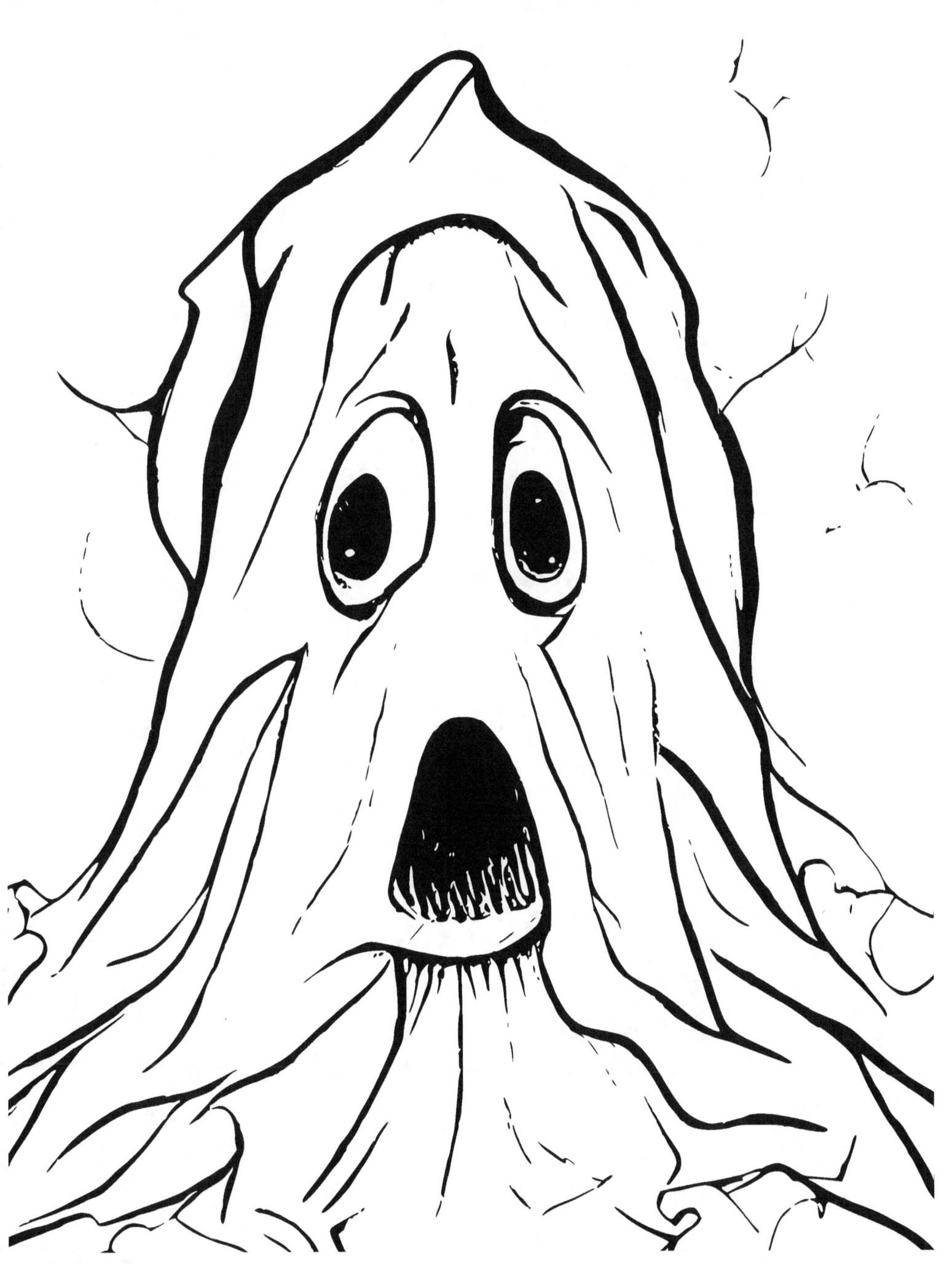

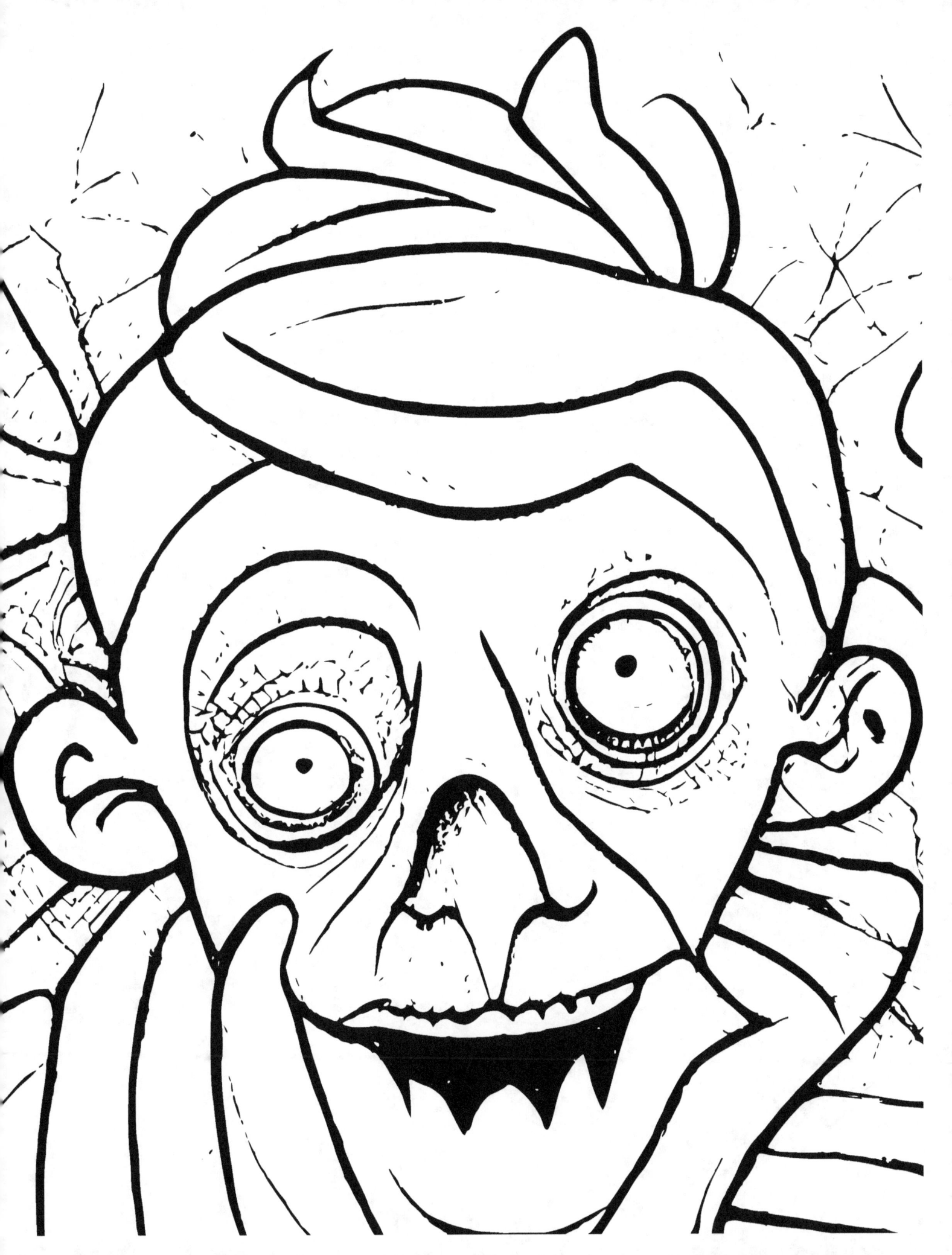

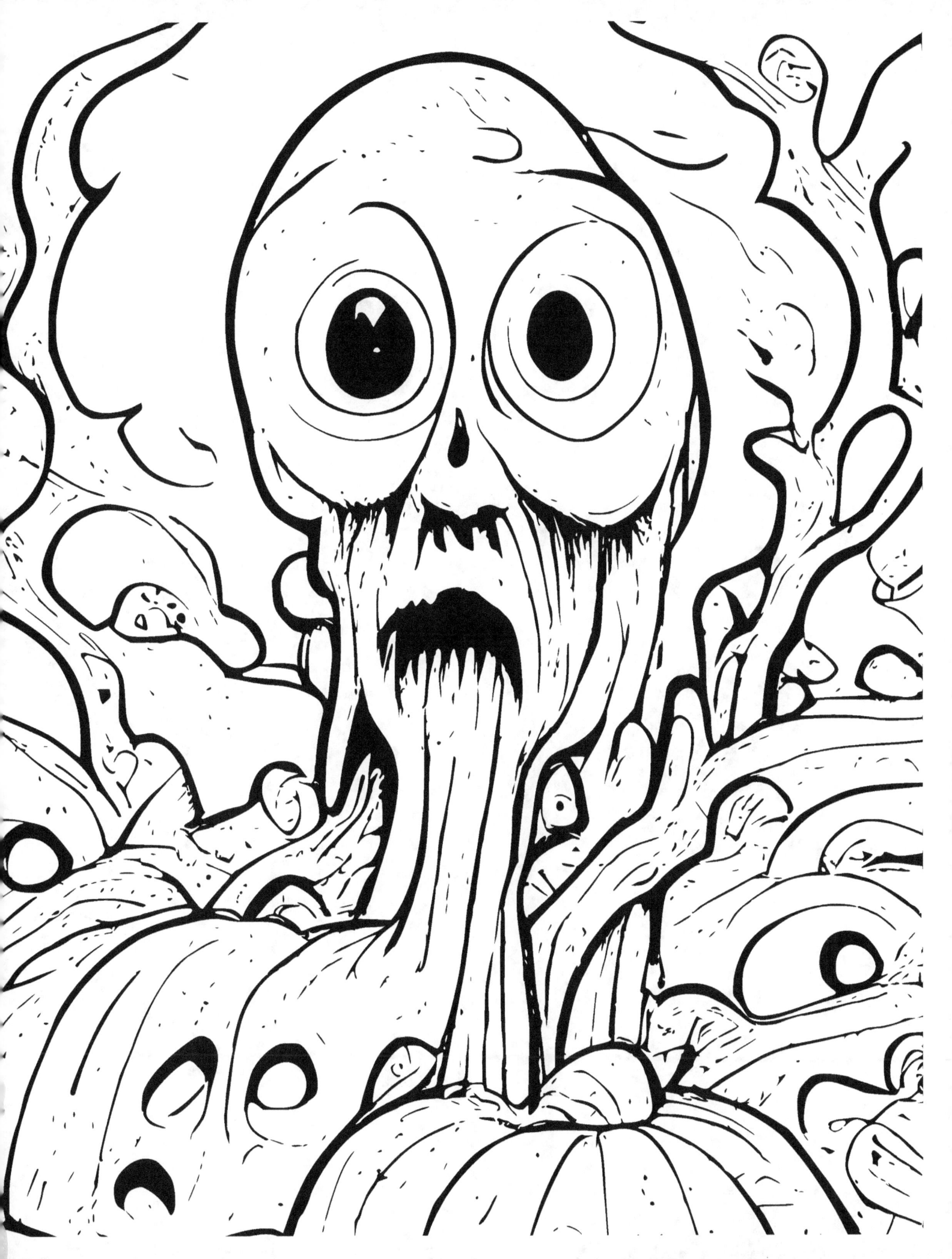

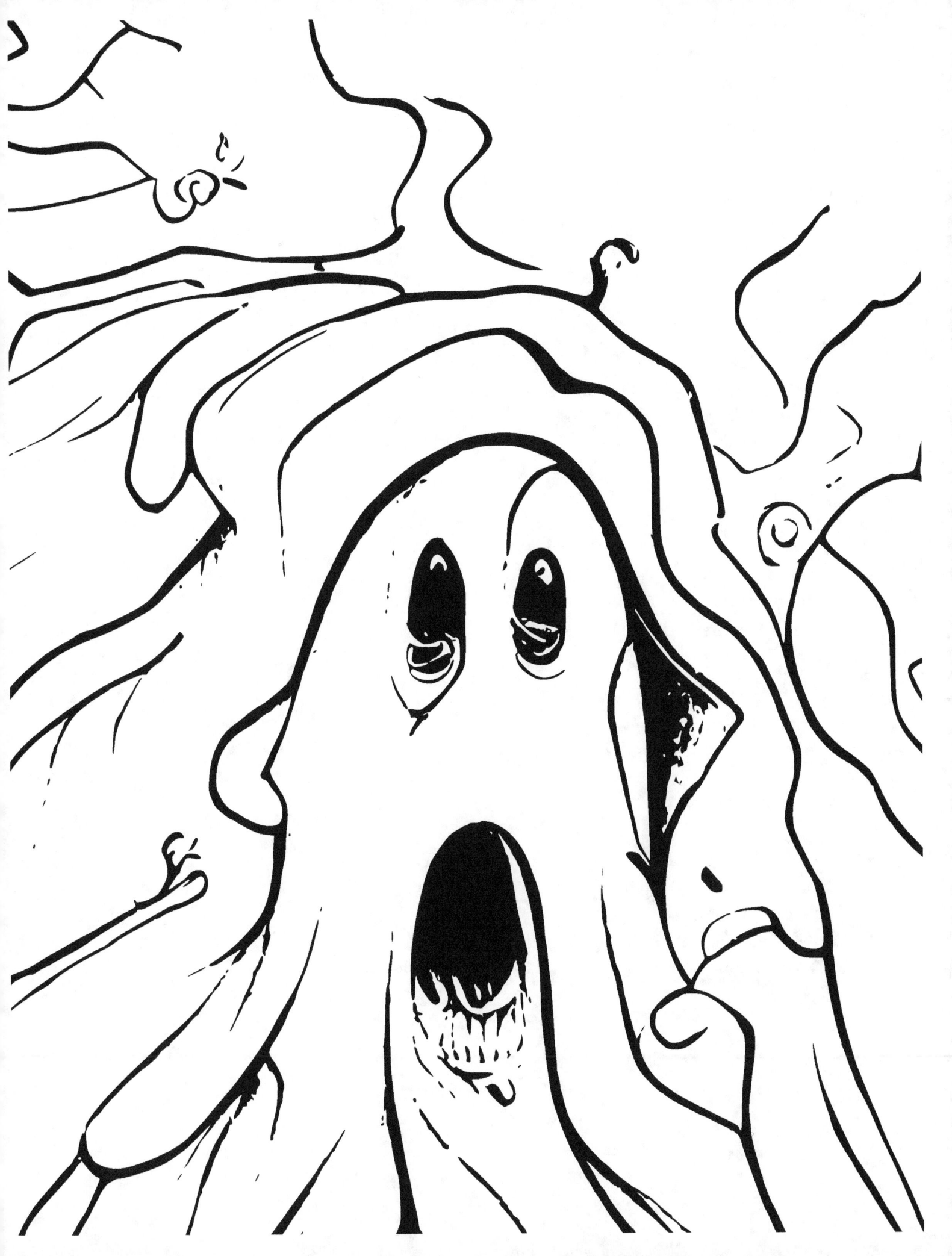

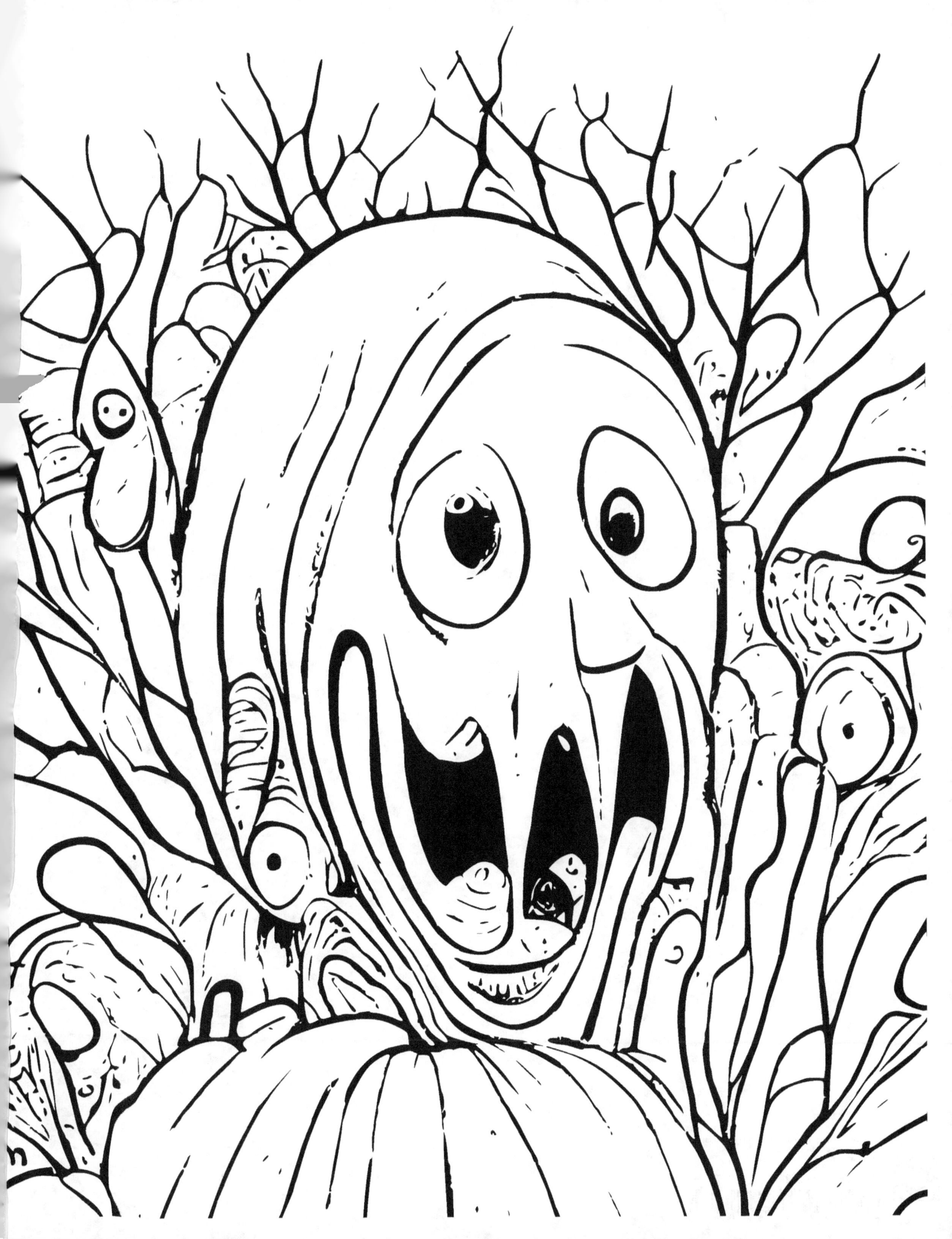

www.ingramcontent.com/pod-product-compliance
Lightning Source LLC
Chambersburg PA
CBHW080508220526
45465CB00006B/2411